Love Your JOURNEY

a curation of self growth
inspiration, scripture, and action

Love Your Journey: a curation of self growth, inspiration, scripture, and action

ISBN: 978-0-578-35366-1

Self-Help / General
Self-Help / Emotions
Self-Help / Personal Growth / Success

Edited by: Heather Felty, Publisher and Founder of Inner Peace Press innerpeacepress.com

Cover Design: Tricia Keightley

For information on purchasing more copies visit

LOVEYOURJOURNEY.CO

This book is dedicated to my amazing kiddos who light up my life in so many ways.

Maci, Kena, and Jackson
aka Maci Lou, Kena Wena, and Bubby Bear

Always choose love over fear.

love

fear

CHOOSE YOUR JOURNEY

aka table of contents

INTRODUCTION

Let me be honest. When I get a new book, typically in the mail from Amazon, I start reading and often I find myself skipping the introduction. I want to start by saying: feel free to skip past this and begin your journey! If you would like to know who is compiling this book, read on. I will begin with my eulogy and end with my story and why I curated this book.

My eulogy... what I hope people say about me at my funeral. "Tricia was an inspiration, truly bright light. She always knew what to say to make others feel better and at the very least provided a moment to brighten their day. She was a Christian, a mom, a web developer, magazine publisher, and a hairstylist. If she were here, she would say her biggest flaw was impatience. Oh, and leaving her clean laundry on her closet floor for over a week! There wasn't a moment in any day that she wasn't thinking about doing something to better herself for herself and her family. If it wasn't quoting a book, writing a book, or reading a book, or listening to a podcast, it was getting new web and hair clients. All while going to soccer, volleyball, and changing diapers in the car. She just wanted the best for everyone."

Enough of the sad stuff, although I am not afraid to die as long as my kids are raised. I do have salvation so I have ultimate faith that I am going to Heaven. One suggestion I have is that if you don't know for certain where you would go today if you died, you might want to check with the Big Guy up above. By this I just mean pray about it and I guarantee you will be led in the right direction, if you can open up and listen. I do have salvation so I have ultimate faith that I am going to Heaven. That brings me to my testimony. One of my web clients who has a unique ministry invited me to "Cherish," a women's conference in San Diego. She sent me a text with a link and said just check this out, I would love for you to come and help sell books. I clicked on the link and immediately began to cry.

Happy, excited tears and a lot of them, but I had no clue at all why. I left the tab open on my computer to save it to check out more of the details later. When I opened it for the second time the floodgates opened again. I looked into flights and I had a free one from a Southwest Airlines credit card. It literally cost me $11 to fly roundtrip to San Diego for the conference. At the time I was a single mom of two girls (Maci 10) and (Kena 8). I had a boyfriend, but it wasn't serious at the time.

I arrived in San Diego, which Is one of my favorite places in the U.S. Have you ever just felt as if you belonged somewhere and you feel so free when you are there? That is how I feel when I am near the ocean. The conference kicked off with some amazing worship. At this time I have to admit I still felt a little weird singing out loud and praising God with a full band. When I was with my dad in the summertime we attended the Church of Latter Day Saints (Mormon), if that tells you anything.

There was a speaker named Linda Pesavento who probably has no idea the huge impact she had in my life and my girls' lives. She did what a lot of speakers don't do – she told us to sit in silence for 90 seconds and just listen to what God has to say to you. So I sat there and I heard God speak to me; he said, "MAKE SURE THE GIRLS KNOW WHO I AM, BECAUSE MAN WILL ALWAYS DISAPPOINT" and "BRING HIM BACK TO ME." Before this experience I had felt the Holy Spirit, but definitely never heard God speaking to me. That day I was saved and what that means to me is I wanted nothing more in life than to have a relationship with my Lord and Savior. At this moment I knew I could have faith that Jesus is with me at all times. I knew that I had to find a church to call home. If for no other reason at the moment it was for my girls and making sure that they had the choice in their lives to truly love God. The second part of that was "Bring Him Back to Me." It just so happened that the guy I was dating at reason at the moment it was for my girls and making sure that they had the choice in their lives to truly love God. The second part of that was "Bring Him Back to Me." It just so happened that the guy I was dating at the time knew the bible front to back. He didn't regularly attend church nor did he really live a Godly lifestyle.

He was flying in from New York the same day I was returning from San Diego. Our flights were supposed to land at the same airport about an hour apart, but they ended up landing at the same time. As he drove me home, I told him what God said to me and he actually got pretty offended. That awkward moment passed, and soon after that man became my husband and baby daddy. We still go to the same church, even though we are no longer married. You will hear bits and pieces of our story throughout this book.

I attended many churches over the years and felt that feeling some Christians have about churches – that all they want is my money and I don't need to go to church to have a relationship with God. All it takes is a blink of an eye to change such thoughts. If you are not saved, I strongly suggest next time you are in church and your pastor says to come to the altar and you feel compelled (Holy Spirit), go – and I mean run – before you change your mind change your mind. If you don't know Jesus as your savior then you might opt to say this prayer to your Heavenly Father.

Dear Lord,

I admit that I am a sinner. I have done many things that don't please you. I have lived my life for myself only. I am sorry, and I repent. I ask you to forgive me.

I believe that you died on the cross for me, to save me. You did what I could not do for myself. I come to you now and ask you to take control of my life; I give it to you. From this day forward, help me to live every day for you and in a way that pleases you.

I love you, Lord, and I thank you that I will spend all eternity with you.

Amen.

When I sat at Abundant Life Church after being saved, I felt this amazing sense of peace. I knew without a shadow of a doubt that it is where I am supposed to be every Sunday. I kept and still keep getting this feeling that I am supposed to work there. I don't know if that means actually working there or the part about being an active minister for God.

"The quality of your life is the quality of your habitual emotions!"

~Tony Robbins

I added this quote because you should be aware of the emotions that keep coming up in your life. If they are negative we need to figure out why. We also need to figure out the best ways to get you back on a positive track and not be suffering in these same patterns. I believe that all the emotions we experience are present because of something that has happened in the past.

I want this book to be a daily resource of scriptures, inspiration, and ways to move out of the past and into the present.

I would highly suggest reading any of the books mentioned in this book!

The more you can stay in the present moment and not worry about the past or the future the better off you will be.

One thing moving forward that I'd ask you to think about is why you are feeling a certain emotion. If you are mad I want you to really think about why you are mad and go through the six steps of dealing with that emotion. This came straight from Tony Robbins, just reworded a little.

1. How am I really feeling (soften the situation)?
2. Identify and acknowledge and appreciate the message.
3. Get curious about what it has to offer.
4. Feel reassured that you can deal with the emotion.
5. Get certain you can handle it in the future.
6. Take action and use it to change your life.

Do you know what one of the deepest of all human fears is? We are all afraid that if someone truly knew us that they wouldn't love us. Actually the opposite is usually true. If you can be your true, vulnerable, authentic self around someone else they will actually love and appreciate you to the fullest extent.

ABOUT EMOTIONS

"Emotions are chemical consequences (or feedback) of past experiences. As our senses record incoming information from the environment, clusters of neurons organize into networks. When they freeze into a pattern, the brain makes a chemical that is then sent throughout the body. That chemical is called an emotion. We remember events better when we can remember how they feel. The stronger the emotional quotient from any event–either good or bad–the stronger the change in our internal chemistry. When we notice a significant change inside of us, the brain pays attention to whoever or whatever is causing the change outside of us – and it takes a snapshot of the outer experience. That's called a memory." ~ Dr. Joe Dispenza, *Becoming Supernatural,* page 3-4.

Said more simply, our emotions arise because of past situations. Our brain does not know the difference between something that is happening currently and an emotion that is arising because of a memory from the past or a hope or fear about the future.

The stronger your vision for the future, the more your energy is going to draw that vision into reality. Sometimes when I do Tony Robbins priming (showing gratitude for past experiences, grateful for future experiences, and sending love to those around you) or a Dr. Joe Dispenza meditation, I catch myself so caught up in the vision of the future that there are actual tears running down my face. This is some powerful stuff. I know you have heard the saying thoughts become things. I do believe this, but I take it one step further and say that feelings become a reality. The reason behind this is that when you can actually visualize something your brain doesn't know the difference between it being real or just a thought. I would again take this one step further and encourage you to write your vision down and create a vision board.

The vision I see for my future is that my person, soulmate, whatever you want to call my dream guy, is sitting next to me on the beach and we are laughing. We are looking at each other with nothing but pure love in our hearts. I feel safe with him. My heart feels safe with him. We make each other the best version of ourselves. He feels safe with me and his heart is safe with me. (This is 100% going to happen if it hasn't already once this book is published!)

When I get a feeling about something and I get chills, I absolutely know that it is true and I am on the right path. This has happened to me a lot lately and that is how I know I am well on my way to enlightenment, or awakening, or whatever you call it.

"Where would you be without your emotions? If the sum total of all your experiences makes up the tapestry of your life, it is the emotions you have experienced that give the tapestry its color." ~ Dr. Bradley Nelson, *The Emotion Code*, page 3.

This is so true. Our emotions are part of who we are. If you want to be the best version of yourself then you need to learn all about your emotions and where they come from. Did you know that we often have trapped emotions from our ancestors? Dr. Nelson writes about this in his book. There is hope and a way to release these emotions. If they stay trapped you often misinterpret situations and get triggered and may not even be able to figure out why. I encourage you to explore your emotions and start to identify if what you are feeling is in the present or from a past memory.

HOW TO USE THIS BOOK

This book was inspired by the Choose Your Own Adventure book series I loved reading as a child. I loved that I could go back to the same book numerous times and it would still feel fresh, and even if I ended up in the same place sometimes, it was with a different perspective.

The main goal of this book is to support you in getting clear on how you are moving along on your journey through exploring the wide range of emotions we experience along the way. When we have a handle on our emotions, we are better equipped to follow the path God set out for us. This is because we let go of the fear of what is thrown at us by others, and trust in the faith that God has a plan for us. It is a beautiful thing to realize you are on the right path.

You can read this book front to back if you like. Though I would encourage you to pick an emotion that needs your attention today, and start there. After you've explored these emotions and journaled about it (in this book or in your own journal), go then to the next emotion that needs your attention. Some chapters have references to another chapter. In that case, go there next. Or not. This is YOUR journey to LOVE! I encourage you to trust that God will always guide you correctly and learn to listen to yourself when it comes to choosing the next action you take on your journey, or which emotion chapter you read next!

Here's to falling in love with your journey!

ALONE

INSPIRATION

You can be just as lonely in a relationship as you can if you are single. I have been there many times. I would much rather feel alone and actually be alone than in a relationship where the other person isn't meeting my needs.

If you get really good at being alone and learn to love spending time with yourself then it makes it much easier to let someone love you. It also helps when you get to know yourself better and you can express to your partner how you want to be loved.

This is one of my all time fears. I don't want to be "alone" for the rest of my life. I do believe that my person is out there and the more open I am to receiving him the sooner it will happen.

I also am fearful of being in a relationship and feeling stuck, which is worse than being alone. This is why even at nearly 40 I definitely know what I am looking for. Keep your head up and have faith that this too shall pass and the future is much brighter.

When you have no one who "loves" you, it is your chance to truly love yourself. This is so true. I know that my time spent alone has been to better my relationship with myself. I also know that I won't feel alone in my next relationship. I have gotten so much better about expressing myself and my true feelings that if this feeling starts to creep up again I will be able to ask for what I need.

SCRIPTURE

Fear not, for I am with you;

Be not dismayed, for I am your God.

I will strengthen you,

Yes, I will help you,

I will uphold you with My righteous right hand.

~ Isaiah 41:10

ACTION ITEM(S)

1. Write a list of all of the things that you have the freedom to do when you are by yourself.
2. Challenge - Go out to eat by yourself and enjoy the solidarity.
3. Challenge - Go see a movie by yourself. This is on my bucket list.
4. Make a list of the things you need and want in a great relationship. If you are in a relationship share this with your partner.

ANGRY

INSPIRATION

You are a product of your habitual emotions. The more that you are angry the more you are going to be angry. It sounds obvious, but the fact is if you don't learn how to deal with being angry all of the time it will deal with you eventually. As humans we tend to keep going back and repeating the same unhealthy patterns. Everyone knows the saying that the definition of insanity is doing the same thing over and over again and expecting different results. So why in the world do we keep getting angry over the same things?

I just realized after listening to a podcast with Lewis Howes and Dr. Joe Dispenza that even though we aren't even thinking about it, we try to recreate the emotions from a past situation. This week I realized something about the man who I thought was the love of my life for a very short period of time – every time he would try to waltz back into my life I would let him. What was I doing? I was most definitely addicted to the emotion of disappointment. After listening to this podcast I started changing as much about my life as possible. I got off of dating apps because I started realizing that those were a form of addiction to attention. We have to stop and take a look and make a shift, even if it is minor. I am also very proud to say that I finally didn't even respond to that old boyfriend, because I know that he doesn't make me the best version of myself. Sometimes you just have to block people so you aren't even tempted to acknowledge them.

SCRIPTURE

So then, my beloved brethren, let every man be swift to hear, slow to speak, slow to wrath; for the wrath of man does not produce the righteousness of God. ~ James 1:19-20

ACTION ITEM(S)

1. Take a deep breath.
2. Identify what is actually triggering you to be angry.
3. Acknowledge and appreciate the message behind the trigger.
4. Get curious about what the situation has to offer.
5. Feel reassured the next time this situation arises that you will be more adept at dealing with it.
6. Get certain you can handle it in the future.
7. Take action and change your life to avoid this in the future.

"We are all just a bunch of mirrors walking around."

"What this means is that the characteristics that we see in other people are reflected back to us. You need to consider "why are they making me angy?" What is it about them and how is this showing up in me?"

~ Rachel Watkins, Live Your Raw Life

ANXIOUS

INSPIRATION

Anxiety is so prevalent in our society. I am a huge believer that the more you say "I have anxiety," the worse it is going to get. The more it becomes an excuse for just not dealing with life, the worse it will get. I have been surrounded by people who complain about anxiety my entire adult life. We make up a lot of our own problems in life in our own heads. It comes from fear, which causes anxiousness about situations. One of the first self help books I read was called The Untethered Soul: The Journey Beyond Yourself by Michael Alan Singer. It talks a lot about our minds and how we cause most situations to happen with our overactive minds. Most often the scenario we create in our heads doesn't even come to fruition. Just like anything else that doctors are overprescribing medication for, if you can get to the root cause of the issue, medication will not be needed. Going through the healing process with a therapist or an energy healer is very tough. It brings up a lot of old issues that haven't been resolved. I had a panic attack while sitting at work one day when I was in the thick of doing EMDR. EMDR stands for Eye Movement Desensitization and Reprocessing. EMDR changes the neural networks in the brain to not have such harsh triggers to traumatic situations. EMDR is an amazing tool for PTSD and I am not just talking about military veterans. I am saying for anyone who has had trauma in their life. I am going to guess that 99% of us have been in some situation or another.

"The bottom line is, you'll never be free of problems until you are free from the part within that has so many problems." ~ Michael Alan Singer, *The Untethered Soul,* page 15.

SCRIPTURE

But those who wait on the Lord Shall renew their strength; They shall mount up with wings like eagles, They shall run and not be weary, They shall walk and not faint. ~ Isaiah 40:31

Have I not commanded you? Be strong and of good courage; do not be afraid, nor be dismayed, for the Lord your God is with you wherever you go. ~ Joshua 1:9

Therefore I tell you, do not worry about your life, what you will eat or drink; or about your body, what you will wear. Is not life more than food, and the body more than clothes? Look at the birds of the air; they do not sow or reap or store away in barns, and yet your heavenly Father feeds them. Are you not much more valuable than they? Can any one of you by worrying add a single hour to your life? And why do you worry about clothes? See how the flowers of the field grow. They do not labor or spin. Yet I tell you that not even Solomon in all his splendor was dressed like one of these. If that is how God clothes the grass of the field, which is here today and tomorrow is thrown into the fire, will he not much more clothe you—you of little faith? So do not worry, saying, 'What shall we eat?' or 'What shall we drink?' or 'What shall we wear?' For the pagans run after all these things, and your heavenly Father knows that you need them. But seek first his kingdom and his righteousness, and all these things will be given to you as well. Therefore do not worry about tomorrow, for tomorrow will worry about itself. Each day has enough trouble of its own.
~Matthew 6:25-34

Anxiety weighs down the heart of a man, but a good word cheers it up.
~ Proverbs 12:25

ACTION ITEM(S)

1. Deep breathing - Inhale slowly and deeply through your nose, shake it out and relax your body, specifically your shoulders, exhale slowly through your mouth while keeping your jaw relaxed, try to keep your breathing as even as possible taking in as much air as you can and exhaling as much air as you can.
2. Write in your journal – daily. When writing, always try to stay positive and turn those negative feelings into gratitude. The more thoughts you can get out of your head the better! There is always and I mean always something to be thankful for.

"So if we want to change some aspect of our reality, we have to think, feel, and act in new ways; we have to "be" different in terms of our responses to experiences. We have to "become" someone else. We have to create a new state of mind we need to observe a new outcome with that new mind."

~ Dr. Joe Dispenza

AWKWARD

INSPIRATION

If you are feeling awkward in a situation it is most likely you making it that way. I learned this actually on a date. The guy I was with said "what do you do about awkward silence?" It used to make me so uncomfortable until this particular conversation. So we literally sat there and stared at each other for like 30 seconds. Guess who was awkward and it wasn't him? It taught me that when you are with another person it is ok to have silence while you digest what they are saying. Actually, it is respectful to be listening and not thinking about what you are getting ready to say. You will be able to pay attention to their words and feelings if you aren't trying to think of a comeback or a reaction while they are talking.

Awkwardness stems from **INSECURE** so might I suggest you skip to that chapter next.

SCRIPTURE

Do nothing from selfish ambition or conceit, but in humility count others more significant than yourselves. Let each of you look not only to his own interests, but also to the interests of others.
~ Philippians 2:3-4

ACTION ITEMS

1. Next time you are talking with someone, just sit and listen to them and don't respond to what they say immediately. Let them finish talking and then respond. (Remember if it gets awkward you are the one making it that way.)
2. See if you can sit in silence with a friend or on a date just looking at each other without it being awkward.

"Silence is beautiful, not awkward.
The human tendency to be afraid of
something beautiful is awkward."

~ Elliot Kay

BEAUTIFUL STATE

INSPIRATION

One way to stay in a beautiful state all of the time is to not suffer from situations in your life caused by others. People talk about boundaries and getting rid of the toxic people in your life. I am not going to mention any names, but there are toxic people in my life who I choose to not let affect me. Yes, I do believe in boundaries, but I also believe it is possible to not let others' decisions, reactions, or actions affect your life. People are always going to disappoint you when you have expectations for them. Step 1: Get rid of those expectations. No one, and I mean no one, is ever going to do what you want them to do all of the time. It would be absolutely boring if they did. Then we would all be the same and life would be way too easy and boring. Step 2: When someone does something that you don't like or hurts your feelings, stop and realize that odds are it isn't even about you and they definitely didn't do it on purpose. Most people aren't cruel on purpose. At least I would like to believe this.

To stay in a beautiful state or get back into a beautiful state my number one go-to is loud music, singing, and dancing. I even sometimes do this in my car and I don't care who is watching. Tony Robbins calls this changing your physiology. Any type of active movement can change your physiology. Go for a run, walk, do something you love and you will no doubt see a shift in your mood.

SCRIPTURE

Pleasant words are like a honeycomb, sweet to the soul, and health to the bones. ~ Proverbs 16:24

ACTION ITEM(S)

1. Create a playlist on your phone for times when you are not feeling in a beautiful state.
2. Write in your journal about what might have happened to make you feel a little more down that day.
3. Play a couple of those great inspiration songs from your playlist and dance in the kitchen or in your car. I promise you will feel better by the time those songs are over. My go-tos are "Simply the Best" by Tina Turner and "Cowboy Take Me Away" by The Dixie Chicks.

BROKEN

INSPIRATION

Remember God will put situations in our lives to bring us closer to him. There have been many times in my life when I have asked, "Why me? Why does this keep happening to me?" I then realize that He is trying to pull me closer. We all have times in our lives when we feel broken. Even saying the words why this keeps happening to me makes it obvious as to why it does. We have to take action in our own lives to be able to move forward. As adults we can't blame anyone for our brokenness except ourselves. Being aware is the first step in self education. Realizing that you are repeating a behavior and then knowing that something MUST change is the second step.

Just because others' lives look amazing and awesome on the outside doesn't mean they don't have bad days and feel broken and lonely. I like to think of the times that I have felt broken as more wounded or bruised instead of broken. When I think of broken things, I think of something that can't be fixed. We don't need fixing, we need healing just like a wound or a bruise.

Don't ever base the value of your life off of someone's instagram feed!

The one thing I will say about this is that the people who feel the need to show off on social media are typically the most insecure. They have their own issues and they are putting their self worth into what their lives and bodies look like. I am a firm believer that when you are confident in your inner and outer beauty you don't need to pose nearly naked on social media or always act like your life is perfect.

SCRIPTURE

Be strong and of good courage, do not fear nor be afraid of them; for the LORD your God, He is the One who goes with you. He will not leave you nor forsake you. ~ Deuteronomy 31:6

ACTION ITEM(S)

1. Make a list of all (at least five) of the things that empower you.
2. Create a mantra list (I'm including mine to provide inspiration).

I AM

free and I have choices

I AM

a hard worker

I AM

able to call the shots in business and in life

I AM

grateful for my circumstances

I AM

responsible and focused

I AM

an action taker making an impact

I AM

the change I want to see in the world

I AM

a constant work in progress

I AM

a pursuer of self transformation

I AM

an amazing mom

I AM

present and available for those who I love

I AM

faithful to my ultimate purpose

I AM

in control of my thoughts

I AM

overcoming my limiting beliefs

I AM

an amazing life partner

I AM

impacting entrepreneurs globally

I HAVE

time and financial freedom

I HAVE

the ability to be the best version of myself everyday

"A mantra is nothing more than a collection of words strung together to create a positive effect."

~ Robin S. Sharma

"The Mantra may be used in any life situation and even during our daily routine to relax and quieten the mind. It will bring clarity and the ability to think positively."

~ Sri Tulsidasji

BROKENHEARTED

INSPIRATION

If you listen to the most inspirational people you will start to realize that they have some of the toughest stories. I have met quite a few people in my life who have had extremely traumatic experiences as children. I have been very close to these individuals. I was always told like attracts like and so at one point about a year ago I started realizing I was attracting very traumatized men into my life. I started going to an amazing counselor. We started digging into my past and I started realizing that the little Tricia in me was still hurting pretty bad. I had done some EMDR (which has helped me learn so much about myself) and had done quite a bit of counseling in addition to reading and listening to every self-help book and podcast possible. One big thing I discovered on my healing journey is that I learned as a child that love is supposed to hurt. If it didn't hurt then it wasn't really love. Which means I was attracting a roller coaster of a life. I mean isn't make up sex the best after you have gotten into a huge fight? If you feel like you need to heal from some past trauma please ask for help from a therapist or some of my most healing moments have been from energy healers.

"The brokenhearted are indeed the bravest among us-they dared to love, and they dared to forgive." ~ Brené Brown, *Rising Strong: How the Ability to Reset Transforms the Way We Live, Love, Parent, and Lead*, page 142.

SCRIPTURE

He heals the brokenhearted and binds up their wounds.
~ Psalm 147:3

The Lord is close to the brokenhearted and saves those who are crushed in spirit. ~ Psalm 34:18

ACTION ITEM(S)

1. Learn to love yourself. Go to the **SELF LOVE** chapter.
2. Write down 10 things you love about yourself. Can be physical, emotional, or personality traits.

CODEPENDENT

INSPIRATION

One of the biggest struggles we have is depending on others for our happiness. We have to learn how to be happy with ourselves and, as cheesy as it sounds, to love ourselves. I mean everything about yourself. This is hard and it is a daily task, but staying positive and grateful for your talents, strengths, weaknesses, beauty, and being full of love brings you to a state of self love. The reason you are full of love is because God is love so how can you deny being made in His image.

"The ego makes us think we need another person, when in fact we are complete and whole as we are." ~ Marianne Williamson, *A Return to Love*, page. 111.

The first step here is realizing that you have codependent tendencies. If you can answer yes to most of these then it may be an issue:

- Are you reluctant to trust others?
- Do you doubt yourself when making decisions?
- Are your moods often controlled by those around you?
- Are you afraid of being alone or abandoned?
- Are you afraid of change?
- Do you have low self esteem?
- Do you carry other people's burdens?
- Do you do more than is required to impress others and earn approval?
- Do you neglect your own needs when taking care of someone who won't take care of their own needs?
- Do you enable others and let them take up your time without your willing consent?

SCRIPTURE

Trust in the Lord with all your heart,
And lean not on your own understanding. ~ Proverbs 3:5

ACTION ITEM(S)

Steps to start to overcome codependency:

1. Think about yourself and write down your dreams, desires, thoughts, and feelings. Where/How do you envision yourself in five years?
2. Start doing things you love doing on your own. You don't have to be around others all the time. Do one activity today that is only for you, by yourself.
3. Go to the **SELF LOVE** chapter.

CONFUSED

INSPIRATION

"When we decide to own our stories and live our truth, we bring our light to the darkness." ~ Brené Brown, *Rising Strong*, page 75.

In the past couple of years I have been more confused than ever. Here I am struggling with trying to figure out how I am going to combine my love for personal development with my website and branding agency. During a goal setting workshop I finally figured it out. During that hour "The Soul Setters' Collective" was born, which was launched just three months ahead of publishing this book. We are a community of business owners or wannabe business owners who are loving our personal journey to business success. A collective of growth minded humans. Hopefully by the time you are reading this it is well on its way to helping many humans globally succeed and love their journey the entire way to success.

The second reason I have been so confused is trying to figure out love relationships. One thing I learned through counseling over the last couple of years is that when I was young I learned that love hurts. If it doesn't hurt it is not love. You can imagine where this gets you as an adult. Two divorces down and still up in arms about finding my person. There are probably only a handful of people who are going to help you be the best version of yourself, and you encourage/guide them to be the best version of themselves.

SCRIPTURE

Be alert and of sober mind. Your enemy the devil prowls around like a roaring lion looking for someone to devour. ~ 1 Peter 5:8

ACTION ITEM(S)

1. Get clear about the issue. Write it down.
2. Write a list of pros and cons if it is a decision you are trying to make.
3. Pray and ask that you will be guided in the direction that God would want you to go. Remember this isn't always going to be the direction you might want. One type of prayer that has been really powerful in my life is sitting very quietly and just listening to what God has to say. You might be surprised at what you hear.

DEPRESSED

INSPIRATION

"A state often caused by 'anger turned inward' at the self. Inability to feel joy or excitement. A low energy, negative state caused by ongoing negative feelings." ~ Emotion Code app

I love this definition of depressed. I had never thought about it this way before and it makes total sense. Depression is absolutely caused by negative feelings. I have been very close to a couple of people who would get really down. This excerpt is written by my sister.

Written by Christine Keightley

Like many others, I have struggled with depression and anxiety for years. I never know when it is going to hit. I don't realize I'm depressed until it's been a couple weeks and I haven't had the energy or motivation to even do the dishes and shower on a regular basis. It takes time for it to click that something has been wrong. I'm sure many of you have had this happen. A slump of darkness that takes over without you being able to acknowledge that it's happening.

My anxiety likes to creep up randomly. I could be doing absolutely nothing and my heart will begin to race and my throat feels all tight. I cannot explain why it happens and what causes this. I'll feel severely overwhelmed and I just have to tell myself it will be okay and that nothing is wrong. It doesn't fix it, but I know I'll get through it.

What I do personally to try and pull myself out of the depression slump (once I realize what has been going on, of course) is to just get up. I have to get up and shower or do the dishes or clean. I have to do SOMETHING. Picking up the pieces after a depressive episode is difficult. The laundry TLC, and you have to reach out to your friends you haven't spoken to for a week because you just didn't feel like talking. I've tried medication, and it doesn't seem to help me, in fact, it makes me feel numb. I don't feel any emotions. However, do not let my experience hinder you from doing this for yourself. Please reach out to a health professional if this is an option for you. I do try to workout on a regular basis, but this does not prevent depression for me. In fact, I need the energy to get up to workout and when I'm depressed, I just don't have that extra umph. *For anxiety, I generally like to be by myself. Being with a lot of people when I'm having an anxiety attack makes it worse. I like to take a hot shower to try to regulate how I feel. If this isn't an option, I try to find a spot where no one can bother me.*

I want to stress to you: YOU ARE NOT ALONE IN THIS. Unfortunately there are millions of people who struggle with anxiety and depression. I wish I could tell you that there is a magic trick to make it disappear but there isn't. Reach out to an understanding friend or family member and talk if you're feeling alone or feeling that you might act in an unsafe way. Having a support system has been one of the most comforting solutions for me.

End of excerpt written by Christine Keightley

"Rest in the assurance that what God has empowered you to do with your mind is more powerful and effective than any medication, any threat, any sickness, or any neurological challenge." ~ Dr. Caroline Leaf, *Switch on your Brain*, page 33.

SCRIPTURE

For God has not given us a spirit of fear, but of power and of love and of a sound mind. ~ 2 Timothy 1:7

And do not be conformed to this world, but be transformed by the renewing of your mind, so that you may prove what the will of God is, that which is good and acceptable and perfect. ~ Romans 12:2

ACTION ITEM

1. It is all about gratitude here. At the same time every day, write down five things you are grateful for right now. It works best for me to do this first thing when I wake up because it will typically brighten my mood for the day.
2. Write down at least five things that bring you joy and excitement. Do this every day until you start feeling more grateful for this amazing life you have been given.
3. Jay Glazer has three steps to help him get unstuck.
4. Find a team of people to help you and ask them for help.
5. Be of service to others
6. Laugh - he has a list of practical jokes that he plays on people and he laughs.
7. If you are feeling more than depressed and feeling **SUICIDAL** please go to that chapter.

"I found that with depression, one of the most important things you could realize is that you're not alone."

~ Dwayne Johnson

"I am bent, but not broken. I am scarred, but not disfigured. I am sad, but not hopeless. I am tired, but not powerless. I am angry, but not bitter. I am depressed, but not giving up."

~ Anonymous

DESPERATE FOR LOVE

INSPIRATION

I've been on a lot of dates, most of them with a new/different person. I am picky and I know what I want and don't want. This doesn't mean that I am not oddly attracted to someone who challenges me to my core. Desperation is hard to admit. There were times when I felt desperate to find love. One thing I know is that in the past I have settled for men who were good looking on the outside and very traumatized on the inside. The main thing this taught me was that I was still on my healing journey. Let me share some important advice: if you are attracted to partners who are mentally and/or emotionally abusive you might want to figure out what you need to heal from. Somehow we are very attracted to people who are similar to one of our parents. This is typically the parent who caused some sort of turmoil in your life. I can honestly say that in my history of men this is most definitely true.

It is 100% normal for you to crave intimate love with a partner. Don't let anyone ever tell you otherwise. The only thing I will ask in this situation is, "are you living the life that the person you want in your life is living?" What I mean by this is if you make a list of 20 qualities that you envision your person having, do you inhabit all of these qualities? I have spent the last six months of my journey making this a reality. I started making my bed, making sure no matter what I brushed my teeth and flossed morning and night (well... floss at least a few times a week), remained on my growth and healing journey, built amazing relationships with friends, hung up my laundry, etc. Just be the person you would want to be with and your vibrations will align much sooner.

"Looking for Mr. Right leads to desperation because there is no Mr. Right. There is no Mr. Right because there is no Mr. Wrong. There is whoever is in front of us, and the perfect lessons to be learned from that person." ~ Marianne Williamson, *A Return to Love,* page 125.

"The ego tells us that there is some special person out there who will make all the pain go away." ~ Marianne Williamson, *A Return to Love,* page 111.

Desperation also stems from comparing your life to others. Let me ask you one thing: Do you envy most of the love relationships you see around you? I know I don't. I know probably two really, truly happy couples. Instead of comparing my lack of a relationship to theirs, I feel deeply happy for them. I am also happy and grateful that I value their relationship and I will have my own when the time is right. When my energy vibration is equal to my person. It is going to be one of those relationships that I don't question. If you are questioning whether it is right or not then you are still in fear or the relationship is trying to make you heal from past wounds or trauma. I have definitely experienced this. When you ask yourself, "Why do I keep attracting the same type of people who lie, cheat, control, or fight all the time?" It will help you immensely to take a look inside and seek some healing from an energy coach or some sort of therapist. I have done it all (and I mean it ALL) in the last 10 years. Once your healing journey is behind you, the right person who feels right and you can picture yourself sitting on a park bench holding hands at age 90 together, that is when you know that you are at the end of your love journey. Or should I say beginning with the right person.

SCRIPTURE

Take delight in the LORD, and he will give you the desires of your heart.

~ Psalm 37:4

ACTION ITEM(S)

1. Stop looking so hard.
2. Go to singles events at church – I would do this over online dating anyday.
3. Just be out to meet new friends, get active in something you love and then at least you have the possibility to meet someone who has something in common with you.
4. Heal yourself and learn to love yourself before bringing anyone into your life.
5. Write down what characteristics you are looking for in a partner and become them. Your energy will literally draw them in.

"And then my soul saw you and it kind of went,
'Oh there you are, I've been looking for you.'"

~ Iona Mink

"One day I am going to wake up, roll over on my side,
and kiss the love of my life good morning."

~ Anita Room

EMPTY NESTING

Chapter by Jen DuBois

INSPIRATION

The common signs of empty nest syndrome can be feeling a loss of purpose, emotional breakdowns, frustration over the lack of control, or excessive anxious thoughts about your young adult's safety, health, etc.

Here's the deal... letting our kids go out into the big scary world is absolutely hard and you may feel like a limb has been severed from your body for the first few days or weeks.

However, it's also a huge WIN to you as a parent knowing that you raised a responsible human who gets to create their own life and share their gifts with the world! That's awesome news!

Wherever you may be on the Empty Nest spectrum I am here to tell you to feel the feels and then refocus your energy. Don't get sucked up and stay in the place where worry, anxious thoughts, what ifs, and the worst part... guilt... of all the "coulda shoulda woulda didn't" set up shop in your mental real estate!

My Story as a Newbie Empty Nester

My husband and I have been married 26 years, and our youngest left the nest 26 days ago today. Let me tell you first hand as a new empty nester, it was bizarre and super hard for the first few days.

My husband and I went through and felt all the feels together. I thought I was prepared, but as the days got closer and closer, the feelings got stronger and stronger. It's hard to explain, but nothing prepared me for him pulling out of the driveway for his last time calling this place "home."

Flashback to 2015, we moved our oldest son to college and that was my first experience letting my first of two sons fly from the nest. I was so paralyzed by fear of all of the unknowns, yet so proud and excited for his new adventure!

I was a total ball of tears all the way home from leaving him in a new city, in a new place, and on his own. However, I had to pull myself together to continue raising my youngest son who was still at home, yet knowing I'd have to experience this all over again in a few years, only this time... I wouldn't have any more kids to raise.

So, as my last kiddo honked and waved goodbye, I did my very best to hold back the tears (almost made it), and then my husband and I walked into the house as if we'd both been hit by lightning. We sat down, looked at each other, and my husband said, "Wow... where did the last 20 years go?" Waterworks for the next hour, recalling all of the joy those two boys brought us.

Now here we are nearly a month later, just me and my husband, who haven't been alone like this in over 24 years! So after the tears, the comfort, and long talks, the next question was... "Now what?"

This is where the rubber meets the road, friends! This is where you get to choose the path that leads to your next chapter. You could choose to stay stuck, sad, worried, and afraid of all the things that are 100% out of your control, or you can choose to reignite your life.

My husband and I chose the latter. We have embarked on a new health journey together, we go out on dates, and we've reconnected as a couple.

We talk to both of our sons often. Getting to know our sons as independent young men taking care of themselves, having real jobs, and living the life they are creating!

As an empty nesting mother, I am working on releasing the need to constantly worry about what may or may not happen, what they do or don't do. My job as a parent for chapter one is done. We have given them all the tools, advice, and guidance and now it's up to them to actually utilize them.

We will always be here to love and support them unconditionally, but it's a true gift when you can appreciate and respect the evolution of the parent-child dynamic.

SCRIPTURE

Do not be anxious about anything, but in everything by prayer and supplication with thanksgiving let your requests be made known to God. And the peace of God, which surpasses all understanding, will guard your hearts and your minds in Christ Jesus. ~Phillippians 4:6-7

ACTION ITEM(S)

1. Renew your relationship with your spouse, partner, and/or tribe by trying something new together - have a date night each week taking turns deciding what to do, etc. Now is the time to reestablish a new normal with your spouse or partner together.
2. Refocus on your health and wellbeing. It's time to take care of YOU! Join a gym, schedule the check up you've been putting off, choose healthier foods, journal, meditate, get out into nature, and get to know yourself again.
3. Release the worries and fears for your adult children as well as the guilt, shame, and blame for all the things you felt you did "wrong" as a

parent. It's easier said than done, so be gentle with yourself and allow time to process the feelings. Our children didn't come with a manual and as parents we do the best we can with the knowledge we have at the time. We all wish we knew then what we know now. All the worries in the world won't change a single thing, so be attentive when they come up and try to change it to a behavior you are willing to practice instead. (For example, when you think, "I'm so worried my son hasn't called in two days!" You immediately go into overdrive and imagine him in a ditch somewhere when it turns out he was just getting settled in, making friends, and starting his new normal. You can help yourself through this process by taking a few deep breaths and saying to yourself, "I am willing to practice trusting that my son will call when he gets a chance.")

4. Reignite your passion and purpose! What lights you up? You get to create your best life too! Take a fun class you've always wanted to try, travel, seek out a new hobby, rekindle old friendships, start a dinner club or book club, etc!
5. Restart a new chapter with your young adults by flipping the script. This means giving them the chance to fly without over advising, rather practicing the art of truly listening to what they are saying. Give them a safe place to share without adding extra worries or your two cents. This is their rodeo now!
6. Remember your children will always be your children no matter how old they get, where they live, or what they do. It's ok to call, text, and send them goodies, yet avoid smothering them. Give them room to spread their wings!
7. Reach out for support. This transition is tough and it will take some time to navigate this uncharted territory. Remember, you are not alone! You can gain support from other parents in this same situation, however the goal is to move forward – not to stay stuck in the sadness and codependent blues. As an Empowerment Coach and newbie

empty nester, I am here for you! If you If you are struggling, feeling a loss of purpose, or unable to find yourself beyond being a parent, let's chat! You are not alone and this is just another chapter in the book of life.

Jen Dubois' Bio

My mission is to inspire and empower women who feel stuck or unfulfilled. My intention is to support them in gaining clarity, confidence and creating the life they truly want. Vision: My vision includes empowering, inspiring and impacting the lives of women. As they become more passionate, strong and aligned through our work together they will naturally influence the people around them and change the world for the better. There is no limit to what can happen when we fill the world with healthy, happy and empowered women.

WWW.JENDUBOIS.COM

"You are never too old to set another goal or to dream a new dream."

~ C.S. Lewis

"Letting go helps us to to live in a more peaceful state of mind and helps restore our balance. It allows others to be responsible for themselves and for us to take our hands off situations that do not belong to us. This frees us from unnecessary stress."

~ Melody Beattie

ENERGIZED

INSPIRATION

I have been so very fortunate that on a typical day I have all the energy I need to get done what needs to be done. This is another mindset piece. Most often our mind gives up way before our bodies do. My advice would be to workout, eat well, and very importantly get enough sleep every night. I need a solid eight hours of sleep just to be a good human. Even if you are at a spot in your life where you can't workout due to an injury or surgery, be as active as you can and listen to your body. You will know when it is time to stop if you pay attention.

"I'm energized by people who are smarter than I am, people who know things I don't know, people who have experienced things I haven't, people who have men and women of great achievement and extraordinary character and can tell me a little about them. People who have great relationships energize me. People who have achieved extraordinary things energize me. People who know exactly what they want energize me. I am energized by people who are at peace with themselves and their God, people who have learned to live with their inner demons and at the same time shine. People struggling against the odds energizes me. People who are willing to give everything to pursue a dream energize me. Silent heroes energize me. I am energized by people who go out of their way to commit random acts of kindness. People who are starving to become the-best-version-of-themselves energize me."
~ Mathew Kelly, *The Seven Levels of Intimacy*, page 85.

SCRIPTURE

I can do all things through Christ which strengthens me.
~ Philippians 4:13

A joyful heart is good medicine, but a crushed spirit dries up the bones.
~ Proverbs 17:22

ACTION ITEM(S)

1. Get at least eight hours of sleep every night. Your body does better if you are on a consistent schedule.
2. Workout or be active for at least one hour every day.
3. Eat four small meals a day or whatever lifestyle you like to abide by. Just make sure you are getting enough from all of the food groups and making sure that your macronutrients are on point.
4. Since this is an awesome emotion to stay in, I encourage you to make a list of the people and things that energize you.

FAILURE

INSPIRATION

The only time you should ever feel like a failure is if you never even tried or if you didn't work to learn from the situation.

We have to fail in order to learn how to succeed.

I have failed at two marriages and for a while I felt like I had failed my kids in that process also. Though soon after, almost to the day I got divorced for the first time, I started on my self development journey. I called a life coach on my way home from work soon after the divorce was finalized and I told her some of what was going on with me. Her exact words were, "Oh no, you need to go see a therapist, get some EMDR, and some more treatment before you will ever be ready for a life coach." That was literally soul crushing. At that point in my life I'd felt like my past didn't really affect me in a negative way. Boy was I wrong! When I went to see my therapist we did EMDR and some other therapies. EMDR is absolutely amazing for anyone with PTSD or trauma. It doesn't make you forget anything, it retrains your brain so you don't get triggered. This still was definitely not the end of my therapy, on my own or with a therapist. I am sure we will dive deeper into that in another chapter.

"It's only a failure if you don't learn from it." ~ Tony Robbins

SCRIPTURE

Jeremiah, say this to the people of Judah: This is what the Lord says: You know if a man falls down, he gets up again. And if a man goes the wrong way, he turns around and comes back. ~ Jeremiah 8:4

The righteous may fall seven times but still get up, but the wicked will stumble into trouble. ~ Proverbs 24:16

ACTION ITEM(S)

1. Get back up.
2. Set a new specific goal.
3. Move on and write down the lesson you learned from the situation.
4. Don't make the same mistake again. You never know, the smallest adjustment in your plan could make it an ultimate success.

FAITH-FULL

INSPIRATION

I can't imagine living a life without having faith in something. I think that having faith is what gives us hope. I know for sure that there is a God and that he is in me. I have faith that when I die my soul will no longer be in my body and I will be in a much better place than the life we have here on Earth. I do think it is very important to have faith in something. I am not saying that your faith has to be anything like mine. Just make sure you have something you can have ultimate faith in.

If you are feeling like you don't have faith then I would start to explore this. I am not here to tell you that there is one church to go to or one thing to have faith in. That is your journey to figure out. I would try to visit different churches or if church isn't your thing download a bible app and try a bible plan. Faith is all about how you feel and not necessarily knowing for a fact something is real. If you go to a certain church and it doesn't feel right then that isn't your place right then. I will tell you that when I went to my church for the very first time it was while I was married and I wasn't in a great place when it came to church. I didn't like it at all. The whole sermon was about money and how much we should be giving the church. I just sat there and thought: Seriously?! a whole sermon on money? WOW! Now after waiting a few years and then going back I love it and can totally appreciate that the church needs money to operate and they do so many amazing things all over the world I have no problem tithing as much as I am able to.

Again if church isn't your thing try a bible app. Or if a bible app isn't even your thing, surround yourself with faithful people and maybe a little bit of that will rub off on you also. We aren't meant to go at things alone. Surround yourself with growth minded people and you won't be able to not watch them and grow with them.

SCRIPTURE

Now faith is the substance of things hoped for, the evidence of things not seen. ~ Hebrews 1:11

ACTION ITEM(S)

1. Write down some things you don't have absolute faith in.
2. Write down the things that you are absolutely sure of.

FEARFUL

INSPIRATION

As humans one of our biggest fears is that we won't be loved. My biggest fear is that I will never receive the kind of love that I crave from a partner. I have felt such love before, but in short moments, not consistently, and this was essentially due to others not wanting to better themselves. It is so scary to go through counseling and dive into the deepest parts of ourselves. Another fear that I think is very common is letting people see who you truly are even behind closed doors and them still loving the "real" you. We all have issues and if you say you don't you are lying about other things, too.

If you operate out of fear you will never be able to experience life to the fullest and happiest. If you operate out of lack you will never have abundance. The best way to not be operating out of fear is to appreciate and be grateful for the things you do have and be open to unknown possibilities. You can't live in your past or live too far in the future. It is best to live in the right now and trust you are exactly where you are supposed to be at this very moment in time. It is completely up to you to make the best out of this life. The only person you have control over is yourself, so if you are growing and contributing, life will go in the direction that you want it to be going.

Fear is on the opposite spectrum of love. My biggest fear is that I will be alone. Just getting this out and being aware of it is the first part of the battle. Ever since I was a small kid I have felt alone. I can remember staring out the window as a child, just crying, feeling like no one cared if I lived or died. There were times as a teenager I felt like I didn't have any good friends. I spent some of the most fun times alone just because I didn't engage or actually try to find friends. One of my daughters is this way and I am trying to push her to seek out really good friends. Get rid of the ones who don't better you and find ones who do. I think everyone feels lonely at some point in their lives. As I noted in the **ALONE** chapter, you can feel more alone with someone than without. I have had the best two years of my life being alone with myself; if you are in a relationship where you feel really alone, you should definitely address it with your partner. I believe that if your partner isn't willing to grow, the relationship will probably never work out in a positive way. If you are reading this book I already know one thing about you – that is that you are willing to grow and better yourself. I am so proud of you for doing so!

If you are living in the present moment then you have no reason to experience fear. Fear is based on past experiences and worrying about how they might affect your future. At this very moment think about all of the things that you are grateful for and it will be impossible to be fearful.

SCRIPTURE

Fear not, for I am with you;
Be not dismayed, for I am your God.
I will strengthen you,
Yes, I will help you,
I will uphold you with My righteous right hand. ~ Isaiah 41:10

ACTION ITEM(S)

1. Write down your fears – all of them. Remember a time in your life that might have caused this fear. Make sure your conscious brain realizes you are at a completely different point in your life and even say to yourself, "My old belief is that I fear ...... and my new belief is that I love and appreciate........" For every negative thought, there is a positive it can be changed to. I am not talking about toxic positivity. Feel your emotions and notice the value in the lesson that certain situations have taught you.

FEELING ABANDONED

Chapter by Corey Brown

INSPIRATION

One of my favorite sayings of all time is "I trust the next chapter because I know the author." This small but mighty phrase speaks volumes about the progress I have made to love and trust myself first. A silver lining to being abandoned multiple times in relationships is this: I realized that I need to change and put my well being first.

Past relationships and experiences have taught me that people leave when I make a decision they don't agree with or like. I have lived with a deep rooted fear of abandonment in my relationships and it has been a dark shadow following me for years. A divorce without the support of family or friends. Complete silence from sibling relationships. Unexplained ghostings from close friends. The list goes on and on. But when I finally did the work to place the focus on me, the pattern stopped.

The realization is this: I am not responsible for how others respond to me and my choices. I am not responsible for their behavior. I am not responsible for making sure everyone else is happy. I am responsible for myself. I am responsible for my behavior and happiness. If I don't take action on this first, nothing else will fall into place for me. If I continue to seek relationships where I morph into someone who pleases everyone around me... I will never be ME in my relationships. I will continue to attract the shallow and insecure relationships that have dominated my life in the past. The irony is that the cure to feeling secure in relationships with others starts with me, continues with me, and ends with me. My people pleasing nature was literally giving myself away, in other words abandoning myself. By finally choosing me and putting myself and my well being first, I am beginning to attract real and healthy relationships for the right reasons in the right seasons.

SCRIPTURE

Be strong and courageous. Do not be afraid or terrified because of them, for the LORD your God goes with you; he will never leave you nor forsake you. ~ Deuteronomy 31:6

ACTION ITEM(S)

1. Feel the feelings. Allow yourself to FEEL the emotions. Name them, accept them, and sit with them. Set a timer and simply feel. Emotions don't make us weak, avoiding them does.
2. Mediate. Whether it's for five minutes or 50 minutes, meditation is a powerful tool. Listen to a guided meditation or simply repeat a mantra. There are plenty of resources available online for free. A short and easy favorite of mine is "All is Well" by Gabrielle Bernstein (easily found on YouTube).
3. Create an image of the future you want. I am a visual person and vision boarding has become a valuable tool for me personally and professionally. Just like goals are more successful when written down and posted visibly, we need to SEE regularly that what we want is possible! Mental visualization works in the same way! Take five minutes a day to simply visualize what you want your relationship to look like. Visualize the best version of yourself showing up FOR yourself and in relationships.
4. Write, draw, or paint your story. This can be journaling, art therapy, stream of consciousness writing, or anything in between. Putting pen/marker/paintbrush to paper is a powerful tool to let emotions out of you and begin making space for healing.
5. Therapy. Speaking with someone who can help you organize, process, and recover from feelings of abandonment is a powerful choice in the path to healing.

FORGIVING

INSPIRATION

I have been put in some crazy situations in my life that have taken a lot of forgiveness. Remember that it isn't true forgiveness until you can stop holding something against the other person. First you need to have some grace for yourself and forgive yourself for believing someone's lies or forgive yourself for the decision you made. We all make poor decisions at times. One really great way to base decisions is to ask yourself, "Does this make me a better version of myself?" It is also great to ask this question when you are questioning a decision someone you are in a relationship with is making.

Forgiving yourself is one of the hardest actions to take. I would first apologize to who this certain situation might have affected and apologize to them from your heart. Asking for forgiveness from others is just as important as forgiving them for what they might have done.

Just the other night I told my daughters that I am so very sorry that I have put them in a situation that looked similar to one that I grew up in and I was asking for their forgiveness. Then I was able to do a forgiveness practice with myself and truly forgive myself for the actions I took or didn't take to protect them and myself. It felt amazing and so freeing.

SCRIPTURE

And be kind to one another, tenderhearted, forgiving one another, even as God in Christ forgave you. ~ Ephesians 4:32

For if you forgive men their trespasses, your heavenly Father will also forgive you. ~ Matthew 6:14

Judge not, and you shall not be judged. Condemn not, and you shall not be condemned. Forgive, and you will be forgiven. ~ Luke 6:37

ACTION ITEM(S)

1. Figure out which people in your life need forgiveness. One of these might even be yourself.
2. Write a letter to this person or yourself about what happened and why it should be forgiven. Then burn the letter.
3. Do a forgiveness meditation, like my "alignment coach" Rachel with **LIVE YOUR RAW LIFE** gave me. She has this beautiful meditation where she sings "I forgive you, please forgive me. Bring love peace and harmony. Bring love peace and harmony." She does this for five full minutes.
4. Or you can do the ho'oponopono prayer – I'm sorry, Please forgive me, Thank you, I love you. You can do this for five minutes and truly feel the forgiveness happening in your body for someone else or for yourself.

GETTING MARRIED

INSPIRATION

Let's just say marriage is humbling. When you are single you don't have nearly as much responsibility as you do when you are married. There is another person expecting the best out of you 24/7. The following passage came from a book I read a few years ago and I thought it was pretty funny and spot on. A lot of people go through their 20s thinking that life begins when you get married. I would argue that life truly begins when you find yourself, you have healed from your past, and you are well on your path to the vision of your future life.

"I thought I was a pretty decent guy, and then I got married. Turns out I'm kind of a toolshed. It's easy to be a decent guy when you live in a bubble. But when you step into marriage, your true colors bleed out. It's like squeezing a sponge. Whatever is on the inside comes out, for better or for worse. If there are serious problems in your life, don't expect them to go away when you get married. Usually they get worse." ~ John Mark Comer, *Loveology: God, Love, Marriage, Sex, And the Never-Ending Story of Male and Female*, page 73.

One huge piece of advice I can give you is to let go of any and all expectations you have for your partner. If you have expectations for your partner you will always be disappointed. After all no one is perfect and you can't expect them to act or react the way you would in specific situations.

As far as the following scripture goes I wouldn't want any man or woman to take this the wrong way. It in no way puts man above women or woman above man. Your body couldn't function without your head and your head couldn't function without your body.

SCRIPTURE

Wives, submit yourselves to your own husbands as you do to the Lord. For the husband is the head of the wife as Christ is the head of the church, his body, of which he is the Savior. Now as the church submits to Christ, so also wives should submit to their husbands in everything.

Husbands, love your wives, just as Christ loved the church and gave himself up for her to make her holy, cleansing her by the washing with water through the word,and to present her to himself as a radiant church, without stain or wrinkle or any other blemish, but holy and blameless. In this same way, husbands ought to love their wives as their own bodies. He who loves his wife loves himself. After all, no one ever hated their own body, but they feed and care for their body, just as Christ does the church for we are members of his body. For this reason a man will leave his father and mother and be united to his wife, and the two will become one flesh. This is a profound mystery but I am talking about Christ and the church. However, each one of you also must love his wife as he loves himself, and the wife must respect her husband.

~ Ephesians 5:22-33

ACTION ITEM(S)

1. Make sure that the person you are wanting to marry is willing to grow with you. Some people, out of insecurity, don't want you to better yourself. Also, make them feel very secure that they are welcome to walk this path with you and not separately.
2. Do not think that getting married is going to make anything in your relationship better. If it is not amazing before you get married then marriage might not be the best option. I learned this the hard way!
3. Make your list of must haves in a partner and trust that it is a deal breaker if they aren't currently all of them. Remember these are your

must haves, not your wish list.

4. Pay attention to red flags. I promise you if you don't pay attention to these details it will come back and haunt you. Make sure to stay true to yourself and if it doesn't feel right then it probably isn't.

"I'm selfish, impatient and a little insecure. I make mistakes, I am out of control and at times hard to handle. But if you can't handle me at my worst, then you sure as hell don't deserve me at my best."

~ Marilyn Monroe

"Always grow together, always cheer for one another, always date, always flirt, and always laugh together while dancing in the kitchen."

~ Tricia Keightley

GRIEVING

INSPIRATION

If you have recently lost someone to death or just lost someone in life, grieving is completely healthy and normal. This reminds me of when a dear friend committed suicide. He was a great person who suffered from Bipolar disorder and he just couldn't ever make life work for himself. He had never been married and never had any kids. He accepted Christ into his life in my office with another dear friend of mine two weeks prior to him taking his life. He came to church with me one time and just a few days later I got a phone call from a mutual friend that he was gone. I went to church that next Sunday and as I was praying for him I heard God say, "He is with me." That is all I needed to hear and it felt so peaceful knowing that he was being taken care of in Heaven where he didn't have Bipolar anymore. In Heaven there is no mental illness.

"Grief and sadness can be part of a transformational process, one that should not be automatically labeled negative. Difficult emotions are at times appropriate; they can be exactly what we need to experience in order to truly heal, grow, and get to the other side of our suffering with meaningful lessons learned." ~ Marianne Williamson, *Tears to Triumph,* page 35.

Our emotions and the way we feel have a reason for being present. The best thing to do is sit with them and feel them, then try to figure out where they are coming from. The more self aware you can be with yourself the more you will be able to work through these tough emotions.

SCRIPTURE

So with you: Now is your time of grief, but I will see you again and you will rejoice, and no one will take away your joy. ~ John 16:22

ACTION ITEM(S)

1. Denial and isolation are one of the first stages of grief. Being alone with your feelings is ok, just don't let this isolation go on too long. There are others feeling loss just like you, and it helps to support each other in your grief. Find an empathetic friend who will listen.
2. Anger is the second stage of grief. This is ok too, just sit with your feelings and don't take your anger out on others or on yourself.
3. Bargaining is the third stage of grief. Remember in this instance that this is in God's hands even if you think you can control any part of this situation.
4. Depression is the fourth stage of grief. Sit in this feeling also and realize why it is there. Try to go about your days as you normally would. The person who is no longer present physically in your life would not want you to be sad. Read more in the **DEPRESSED** chapter.
5. Acceptance is the fifth stage of grieving. The best way to get to this stage is to look back on your memories and appreciate the person for having been in your life.

GUARDED HEART

INSPIRATION

I will tell you that I am seriously the best at guarding my heart. I am like a vampire who can literally just shut off my emotions. When I started going to counseling the very first time it was because I never wanted to be as shut down as I was when I first got divorced. I had gotten to the point where I felt so trapped because I had shut off all of my emotions to the situation. I never wanted to feel this way again. I have gotten to this place a couple of times since then. It is so much easier to go through life and act like you don't care than to really sit with your emotions. Another thing I am completely guilty of is that I stay busy as it helps me avoid having to just sit with my emotions and feel them. My sister once said to me, "Tricia, I think you are addicted to chaos." I like to think that I take what people say in most accounts and digest and see how I feel about them. Part of being self aware I guess. After many years of counseling and at least 10 different coaches I can say that I am the most vulnerable I have ever been – and this is a good thing. I probably tell people too much at times. This is my way of staying open and honest with myself and others who I have a relationship with. I show more humility than I ever have before and I still pray that I don't ever have to guard my heart like I have in the past.

The really crazy thing is my first husband never would have hurt me like the other men in my life have. I had absolutely no reason to guard my heart. The problem was I didn't know any better at the time. Another huge lesson that I wish I would have learned sooner is that you should most definitely put your husband first. It gets a little tricky for a second marriage, but for a first marriage with the father of your babies you should put him first. I made the mistake of putting my girls first and brushing him to the side. If you truly want to make your marriage or relationship work, keep dating your husband or wife – plan special time together.

Another small piece of advice: don't let your kids sleep in bed with you. Intimacy in a relationship is so very important and right before you go to bed it is so great to unwind and at minimum ;) talk through how your day was.

SCRIPTURE

And the peace of God, which surpasses all understanding, will guard your hearts and your minds in Christ Jesus. ~ Philippians 4:7

Peace I leave with you; my peace I give to you. Not as the world gives do I give to you. Let not your hearts be troubled, neither let them be afraid. ~ John 14:27

ACTION ITEM(S)

1. Only one action item here. Pray this prayer, "Dear God, please prepare me. Open me up and make me new. Destroy the walls that surround my heart." ~ Marianne Williamson, *Enchanted Love*, page 56.

HABITS

INSPIRATION

One thing I have learned about myself recently is that I am a free spirit. I don't do well with creating new habits unless I make small adjustments daily. I am currently working on making my bed daily. Now talk about a minor adjustment. I have to just pull the covers over and my bed is made. I started this new habit because I heard someone say that the most successful people make their bed daily. For some reason this turned into a must do for me and I have been making my bed on a daily basis for four weeks now. Your pituitary gland releases dopamine while you make your bed and every time during the day when you see that it is made. This happens because you are proud of yourself. This is a minor adjustment that can make such a huge difference.

Another habit I have started is writing in this book. I promised myself that I would work on it for one hour every day, whether that be actually writing or reading to get some inspiration.

If there are habits that you are struggling to make happen, try to make it as easy as possible on yourself. I put a gym in my basement for this very reason. I have some really great friends who own gyms and each is about 20 minutes away from my house. Some people might not understand this but as a single parent with three kids I do a lot of driving to begin with. I know myself well enough to know that I am not going to spend 40 minutes in the car getting to and from the gym. I have a gym membership to a gym that is five minutes from my house. I either go there or I workout in the basement, whatever suits my schedule for that day. I also workout four to five days a week. I won't be hard on myself anymore for not working out every day. It just isn't possible in my life right now and it definitely doesn't seem part of the balance I am seeking. Back to me being a free spirit... I know that I will never be able to work

Monday through Friday from 9 am to 5 pm and do the same things every day. It is just not how I am built. Some people need this kind of structure and generally those are the people who can create habits and stick with them on a daily basis. Then you have the people like me and the most structure I have is that I know where I need to be at certain times and squeeze in other tasks when I have time available. I create a schedule every morning for my day (at least during the week, not so much on the weekends). I time chunk my planner into one and two hour increments to work on projects and this works well for me. I used to be so hard on myself and think I was going to plan entire weeks at a time and that never worked, so I started making it easier on myself to create good habits. I would highly suggest James Clear's book Atomic Habits to give you some good ideas that will work for you.

"Success is the product of daily habits - not once-in-a-lifetime transformations." ~ James Clear, *Atomic Habits*, page 18.

SCRIPTURE

Fix your thoughts on what is true and good and right. Think about things that are pure and lovely, and dwell on the fine, good things in others. Think about all you can praise God for and be glad about.
~ Philippians 4:8

ACTION ITEM(S)

1. Write down your current habits from when you wake up in the morning until you go to bed at night.
2. Which of these habits do you wish you could change?
3. Start today, not tomorrow. We don't need a Monday or a New Years' Resolution to create a new habit.

4. Start one new habit on day one... pick a small habit or a step to creating this habit. For example if you are wanting to start getting healthier then start going for a walk in the morning for even just 15 minutes. You have to start somewhere and the hardest part is starting. If you drink soda, cut it out; if you drink multiple sodas a day only have one. Catch my drift?
5. Once you have succeeded in creating a new habit, start another one. Do not overwhelm yourself with 10 new habits at once.
6. Make your new habit fun. If you love to dance then go get your exercise in a dance fitness class.
7. Make your new habit easy. If you don't like cooking, but you want to start, make it easy for yourself. Secretly (or not so secretly) I have become addicted to TikTok videos on healthy recipes using my airfryer. I cooked dinner every day last week for my kids in 15 minutes or less.
8. Get a habit tracker so you can be proud of your accomplishments and celebrate yourself with something once you have maintained doing something for a full week.

"In essence, if we want to direct our lives, we must take control of our consistent actions. It's not what we do once in a while that shapes our lives, but what we do consistently."

~ Tony Robbins

HAPPY

INSPIRATION

Whether you want to feel happy or you are reading this chapter because you are happy and you want to stay that way, the actions are the same. If your happiness depends on other people or the ifs in your life, then you will never be happy long term. Happiness comes from within. We are all struggling on this planet in some way, shape, or form. Most people can't say that they are a 10 out of 10 on the wheel of life.

As I wrote in the beginning of the book, I like to up the saying "thoughts become things" to say "feelings become reality". If you sit and think about what you envision in your future compared to writing it down and reading it out loud and really, truly feeling the emotion behind how it is going to feel when you get there, then you will genuinely be able to turn feelings into reality.

"I sit here and I picture my soulmate sitting next to me on the beach and we are laughing in between reading and enjoying the sun and the sound of the splashing waves. My kids run up one by one and are having so much fun on the beach. I am a published author and I am truly making a positive impact on people's lives." This is my happy place and sometimes when I say this out loud it literally brings tears to my eyes. The more emotion you have tied to the vision of your future, the faster it will be a reality.

Happiness is a choice. It is not possible to be happy 100% of the time, but if you can focus on appreciation and love, I guarantee that the percentage of happiness in your life will always be higher.

I have learned through my singleness that you have to get to a place in yourself where you are so happy that you stay in a beautiful state no matter what others do. You have to remember, too, that other people aren't doing things to you when they don't meet your expectations. They are just a different person and have different expectations even of themself. You can't depend on anyone to do exactly what you want them to do, especially when they have to read your mind to even know what you expect. This is something that I definitely struggle with. I think women in general struggle with this because we want men to read our minds or think like us. That is never going to happen.

The happiest moments of your life are when you don't care about the past and you aren't worried about the future.

SCRIPTURE

Take delight in the Lord, and he will give you the desires of your heart.
~ Psalm 37:4
Our mouths were filled with laughter, our tongues with songs of joy.
~ Psalm 126:2

ACTION ITEM(S)

1. Gratitude and appreciation will always keep you in a happy place. Write down everything you are grateful for and make sure before each one you write thank you so much for... I want you to say it out loud and truly feel how grateful you are for that situation or person and why.
2. Write down your if/when statements. If so and so does this, I will be happy. When this happens I will be happy.
3. Cross them out and write I am already happy because...
4. Make a list of everything that makes you happy. If you are in a relationship, then you can do these with your partner or friends. If you are single like me then I challenge you to make these happen even if you do them by yourself. Currently I go to dinner by myself. I went to

Cancun by myself last year, and next on my list is going to a movie by myself. The biggest challenge for me is staying in a happy mood while doing these things by myself. The one thing I will say is that I am so much happier doing these things by myself than with the wrong person who I feel lonely with regardless of doing something fun. Just focus on being grateful that you are able to enjoy the happy experience alone or with someone.

"The biggest adventure you can ever take is to live the life of your dreams."

~ Oprah Winfrey

HEARTBROKEN

INSPIRATION

I feel like I have been heartbroken a few times in my life and maybe have even stayed that way for a few months at a time. When I hear the word heartbroken I think of someone as a love interest breaking my heart. I have only experienced sudden heartbreak one time in my life. It was one of those moments that I thought my heart was literally going to stop beating. I was crying so hard I could barely breathe. My person broke up with me and didn't want to see me at all. I could not believe what I was hearing. This was the first time in my life someone had broken up with me. Believe me, I don't think of this as a good thing. I kept myself guarded and I broke up with others before they had the chance to hurt me. This is no way to live. The other times I have experienced heartbreak have been slowly over time. This was by my past partners disappointing me because they weren't living up to my expectations. This is no way to live either. In short, if we have expectations for others we will always be disappointed in some way.

I promise this feeling will subside even though in the moment it is so hard to believe that life can go on without this person in your life. I very much think that people are put in your life for a season, reason, or a lifetime. This person who broke your heart was likely put in your life for a reason to teach you something.

I think I needed this person in my life to help me through one of the toughest times I have ever had. He was also put in my life to trigger me enough to make me realize that I still had a ton of healing work to do. Once you can appreciate the reason the person who broke your heart was put in your life, it makes the grief a little easier. Now I can appreciate this situation and not suffer from it or dwell on it anymore at all.

SCRIPTURE

The LORD is near to those who have a broken heart, And saves such as have a contrite spirit. ~ Psalm 34:18

ACTION ITEM(S)

1. Go to the **GRIEVING** chapter because that is probably how you are feeling.
2. List a time when you were heartbroken and what lesson you learned from it in hindsight.

HOPEFUL

INSPIRATION

I am so glad you are feeling hopeful today. If you are reading this chapter because you want to feel hopeful then "hopefully" (pun intended) the action items will get you in a hopeful state of mind. The world we live in can take a turn real quick so if you want to stay in a hopeful state you can write down what you are excited about every single day. The way we spend the first 30 minutes of our day is so very important. I spend mine meditating and sometimes even journaling. Being grateful and appreciative of everything we have in our lives, even the small things, can completely change our ways of thinking and ultimately our lives.

I have always been blessed with hope. I think that we are all blessed with hope because that is one of the things the Holy Spirit provides for us. I think hope stems from having faith that life is always going to get better.

"Don't measure the size of the mountain; talk to the One who can move it. Instead of carrying the world on your shoulders, talk to the One who holds the universe on his. Hope is a look away." ~ Max Lucado, *Begin Again: Your Hope and Renewal Start Today,* page. 14.

SCRIPTURE

And do not be conformed to this world, but be transformed by the renewing of your mind, that you may prove what is that good and acceptable and perfect will of God. ~ Romans 12:2

ACTION ITEM(S)

1. You have to have hope for your future, or depression sets in. If you want to stay in a hopeful state I would say one of the best ways to do this would be to write down everything you are excited for in your future.

2. Kind of like the quote from The Four Agreements (see below), start by envisioning your future. Write it down with the smallest of details so you can really start to feel the emotions that this amazing future brings up for you. If there are any negative thoughts that arise, set them aside and think about how you deserve to have everything this world has to offer.
3. Create a vision board with all of your hopes and dreams on it with pictures and put it somewhere where you will see it on a daily basis.

"Using your imagination and your new eyes of perception, I want you to see yourself living a new life, a new dream, a life where you don't need to justify your existence and you are free to be who you really are."

~ Don Miguel Ruiz, *The Four Agreements*, page 124.

INSECURE

INSPIRATION

I think being secure in yourself just comes with time. I think we go through a phase around third or fourth grade when we start to not just be friends with everyone and are actually worried people will reject us. Often insecurity stems from our parents not accepting who we are. Self worth can be another term for insecurity. There are so many things that go into being more confident and secure as a person. I didn't feel like I hit my stride of being really confident in who I am and really appreciating myself until I was probably 37 years old. My first step was forgiving myself for all the stupid decisions I had made up until that point. My second step was seeking counseling to try to heal from some past trauma. My third step was learning to practice self care which we go into more in the SELF LOVE chapter. If you don't take care of yourself, who will? I always talk about the airplane oxygen mask example. If you have your kids and husband or wife sitting next to you, who's mask are you going to put on first? If you don't put yours on first and pass out while trying to get one on your kids then you are screwed. If you put yours on first then you will be able to help your kids and possibly even your husband or wife. We can apply this same theory to life. If you get home from work and you need 15 minutes to just chill, then take it. If you want to take a bath in the evening, take it. Trust me, everyone in your house will be much happier if you aren't on edge all night because you didn't take a little time for yourself.

SCRIPTURE

If God is for us, who can be against us? He who did not spare His own Son, but delivered Him up for us all, how shall He not with Him also freely give us all things? ~ Romans 8:31-32

ACTION ITEM(S)

1. Put your mask on first... take a bath, meditate, journal, do some breathwork. If you can, make a deal with your partner that you each get 30 minutes of quiet time away from the kids after work. This is especially important if you are a stay-at-home parent. You deserve an hour at least every night to take a break from your daily household responsibilities. If your significant other knows you need an hour to just chill so you can be in a great mood the rest of the night, I bet that would be a no brainer.
2. Make a list of the situations when you feel the most insecure. Sometimes this comes from our parents. I would say being around a bunch of beautiful women used to make me feel insecure until I started valuing myself.
3. Read the **MASCULINE AND FEMININE** chapter and see if you can relate to the mother and father wounding.

IN YOUR HEAD

INSPIRATION

"Your inner growth is completely dependent upon the realization that the only way to find peace and contentment is to stop thinking about yourself." ~ Michael A. Singer, *The Untethered Soul: The Journey Beyond Yourself,* page 15.

The inspiration that I got from this quote and the entire book it comes from is that most of our "problems" aren't even really problems. In situations you see as problems you might ask yourself, "Why is this problem bothering me and what is bothering me about it?" When you can answer this question, you can figure out a way to solve the internal issue that is arising because of the situation.

For instance, your significant other is supposed to meet you at dinner at 7 pm and they aren't there on time. So about 7:15 pm you have a "problem." In your head, you come up with every reason why they aren't there. Mine would likely be something else that is more important than me and is making them late. Maybe this comes from being a middle child who felt like her older sister was always the center of attention, which only got worse when my little brother was born and really took all my parents' attention.

In this situation, if I would have asked myself what the real internal issue is, I would acknowledge that I feel less important than something/someone else. Feeling unseen and unheard is a typical trait that women suffer from.

At 7:16 he shows up with flowers and there is no issue if I realize that the real "problem" is internal. He says, "I am so sorry the line at the flower shop took forever and I tried to make it on time." The bottom line is that if you can learn more about your thoughts/feelings and make sure you don't overanalyze and get beyond the self, that is when you will be free from your problems.

SCRIPTURE

Be strong and of good courage, do not fear nor be afraid of them; for the LORD your God, He is the One who goes with you. He will not leave you nor forsake you. ~ Deuteronomy 31:6

ACTION ITEM(S)

1. Next time a problem arises, ask yourself: "Why is this problem bothering me and what is bothering me about it?"
2. Do a guided meditation. There are plenty of them on YouTube. If you do a guided meditation make sure that if your mind wanders that you come back to the words in the meditation as quickly as possible. Dr. Joe Dispenza is my guided meditation facilitator. The more you practice meditation, the more you can get your mind to calm down and that voice inside your head with negative fearful thoughts will disappear.
3. Make the decision to be happy. Stay in a beautiful state as often as you can. Go to the **BEAUTIFUL STATE** chapter to read more about this.

IRRITATED

INSPIRATION

"Nothing other people do is because of you. It is because of themselves. All people live in their own dream, in their own mind; they are in a completely different world from the one we live in. When we take something personally, we make the assumption that they know what is in our world. And we try to impose our world on their world." ~ Don Miguel Ruiz, *The Four Agreements*, page 48.

I am sure you have heard the saying "It is not about you." This is so very true. How people react to different situations is a direct representation of their past and how they live in the present moment. I would even venture to say that they react because they might be scared of the future.

If you are irritated about how someone else acted in a certain situation, think about this and reorganize your thoughts before you say or do something that will ultimately hurt both of you.

A lot of times your irritation comes from something that is triggering you from your past. I am telling you the first step in figuring out any situation is becoming aware. What I mean by this is if you are aware of why situations bring up certain emotions you are so much more likely to be able to deal with them in a reasonable manner.

SCRIPTURE

Refrain from anger, and forsake wrath! Fret not yourself; it tends only to evil. ~ Psalm 37:8

ACTION ITEM(S)

1. Take a moment of silence for yourself and pull yourself out of the situation.
2. Think about what you are ultimately irritated about.
3. If it is because of someone else's actions reread the quote above.
4. If you are irritated at yourself about something you have done then think about what ultimately made you do what you did. We have to forgive ourselves and have grace for ourselves also. None of us were raised perfectly by perfect parents. We are going to fail, but we can succeed if we learn from those poor choices.
5. Remember that if you have expectations for others you are almost always going to be disappointed. We all grew up different ways and have different thoughts and beliefs. Thank God no two people are exactly the same.

LACK OF INTIMACY

INSPIRATION

The only way to get true intimacy in a relationship is to be vulnerable and show humility when there is a disagreement. When the ego is talking it is hard to back down from a fight. When your true self is talking you are much more reasonable. Next time you are in a fight, let down your pride and take a few minutes, or maybe even hours, to calm down so you avoid saying things you don't mean. I know because I am about as stubborn as they come. My go-to is to shut down and shut off my emotions. I truly do not like this about myself, but that is what I had to do growing up so my situation didn't hurt so bad. This is one of my biggest challenges in the heat of the moment – to back down and be aware of where the other person is coming from.

"Our desire for happiness is ultimately a desire for intimacy. If we have intimacy we can go without an awful lot and still be happy. Without intimacy, all the riches of the world cannot satisfy our hungry hearts. Until we experience intimacy, our hearts remain restless, irritable, and discontented." ~ Matthew Kelly, *The Seven Levels of Intimacy*, page 8.

SCRIPTURE

Better is the end of a thing than its beginning, and the patient in spirit is better than the proud in spirit. Be not quick in your spirit to become angry, for anger lodges in the bosom of fools.

~ Ecclesiastes 7:8-9

ACTION ITEM(S)

1. No matter what, when you see your partner, greet them with a smile and kiss them on the lips.
2. Don't sweat the small stuff. No one is ever going to do everything the way you would do it nor is there anyone who is going to do everything

you expect to be done. Definitely not the way you want it done.

3. Don't try to change your partner. Instead of complaining at them just pray for them to grow in maturity and spirituality.
4. Say you're sorry and mean it. Maybe to go along with the apology, you make his/her coffee the exact way he/she likes it before he/she even gets out of bed. Do something special. The small things can be so huge, especially during an apology.
5. Always speak positively and be grateful for your significant other. Remember thoughts become things and the more good things you can say the better, even if sometimes you don't want to. Always speak out of love. Occasionally praise them for the good things you see they are doing.
6. Don't ever go to bed mad. At least not too mad. Always kiss goodnight at the very minimum and say I love you.
7. The more you show appreciation for the things the other person does the more they will do for you. You will be amazed by how far a little appreciation can go.
8. Praying together is extremely powerful. It is really hard to be this vulnerable and share your relationship with God with someone else and I can't say I have much experience in this arena, but I would say with your significant other it is one of the most important things you can do together.
9. Listen with empathy not sympathy. Don't pull a, "well at least you didn't..." It is much more helpful to say, "oh, I am sure that made you feel..." Empathy is when you actually sit with someone in the pain and try to understand how they are feeling rather than being sympathetic. Brené Brown has an amazing video on this. Look it up on YouTube if you're curious: Brené Brown on Empathy.
10. Make sure that after the argument or discussion is over that the other person truly knows what you need from them moving forward.

LIMITING BELIEFS

INSPIRATION

"We ask ourselves, Who am I to be brilliant, gorgeous, talented, fabulous? Actually, who are you not to be? You are a child of God."

~ Marianne Williamson, *A Return to Love*, page 190.

We all have beliefs that hold us back. More often than not it is a belief that we won't be loved for who we truly are. It seems like most people I have talked to about limiting beliefs develop them at a very young age. If we can heal and deal with our emotions and just be aware of our limiting beliefs they can typically be overcome. Some of these subconscious beliefs have to be dealt with in a slightly different way. I have done some major energy work recently with a few different coaches. It has been completely amazing. Some of this work seems supernatural and I was just telling my daughters the other day that there is no way that God is the only supernatural thing that exists. I am getting to the point where I believe that most of us are living three dimensional lives and there are actually five dimensions. We only use a fraction of our brain and I truly believe we are capable of so much more. Recently I feel like I have gotten to a place in my healing journey that I started trusting myself and my intuition. This is when my eyes started opening up to my purpose and started leading me down the path of all of my activities in life being things I absolutely love. They are truly lighting my soul on fire. I am getting to help people on their healing journey through this book, my collective, relationship workshops, and even my business.

SCRIPTURE

Be transformed by the renewing of our minds. If you can alter the way you think, your life can radically change. If you can identify your Limiting Beliefs or Ungodly Beliefs, you can rewrite them as Godly Beliefs.

~ Romans 12:2

ACTION ITEM(S)

1. Identify your top three limiting beliefs.
2. Write down what negative consequences you have experienced because of these beliefs. Spend at least 15 minutes on this. Go as deep as your mind will allow you to go.
3. Write down what could happen in your life if you no longer believed these things. Be very specific as to how you see yourself without these limiting beliefs.
4. First write down an old belief and right below it right down your new belief.
5. Remember the only time we actually make a change or meet a goal is when we have emotion tied to it.

LOOKING FOR YOUR SOULMATE

A soulmate is someone with whom you connect instantaneously and who accepts you for who you are, loving you unconditionally.

INSPIRATION

If it doesn't feel right then it isn't for you. Listen to that tiny or big voice inside of you. When you are in sync with the universe, you no longer feel the pain, the despair, or the disappointment. You know that whatever is happening is for your highest good. Bottom line is if it doesn't feel right in the beginning then it isn't going to just magically feel right.

I created an entire workbook to get you prepared and your energy aligned with your soulmate. Visit this website to get the workbook completely free **loveyourjourney.co/workbook** I would love for you to download the workbook and share it with all of your single friends who may be searching for their person.

I spent a long time in the wrong relationships. Most of the time I just went with whomever liked me and I was always too scared of rejection to put myself out there for someone I really was crushing on. I have done so much healing work that I truly feel I am ready and any day now my energy is going to completely align and God is going to bless me with the man of my dreams. I believe this 100%! The first module in the workbook I created shares that if you believe it, that is 90% of the battle. The other 10% is really hard internal work, but if you are reading this chapter I assume you are ready and willing to do the work that it takes to better yourself.

SCRIPTURE

Nor was man created for the woman, but woman for the man. For this reason the woman ought to have a symbol of authority on her head, because of the angels., neither is man independent of woman, nor woman independent of man, in the Lord. For as woman came from man, even so man also comes through woman; but all things are from God. ~ 1 Corinthians 9-12

ACTION ITEM(S)

1. Make a list of must have qualities, values, personality traits you would like to see in a partner and then a second list of wishes. Below is mine to give you an idea, but be sure to make it your own.
2. Practice self care. As my dear friend Rachel said, "Tricia you need to take a bath." This was the last piece of my healing journey. I started taking baths, a little longer showers, making my bed, keeping my house more picked up, relaxing and watching TV a little, working out on a more regular basis, yoga, meditation on a daily basis (sometimes twice), pedicures, and best of all just truly taking care of me.
3. What is on your self care top 10 list?

- Honest
- Loyal
- Secure
- Committed
- Thoughtful
- Loves to travel
- Healthy lifestyle
- Personal growth
- Funny
- Faithful
- Open minded
- Positive
- Supportive
- Doesn't overwork
- Financially free
- Soulmate connection
- Good w/ kids
- Conservative
- Accepts me for me
- Responsible
- Confident
- Loves himself
- Listens
- Sexually compatible
- Christian
- Spiritual

LOST

INSPIRATION

When you think about the present it is perfect. At this very moment nothing is wrong if you can forget about the past and quit worrying about the future. Your past does not define you, although it has made you who you are – so own it and appreciate it.

"Make a distinction between who you truly are, the real multifaceted, unique you and the person you have become through toxic choices."
~ Dr. Caroline Leaf, *Switch on Your Brain*, page 45.

If you can see the distinction between the two then you have overcome half of the battle. We are not our choices. We can always make different choices the next time we are faced with a similar situation. Our sins don't define who we are.

"True belonging is the spiritual practice of believing in and belonging to yourself so deeply that you can share your most authentic self with the world and find sacredness in both being a part of something and standing alone in the wilderness. True belonging doesn't require you to change who you are; it requires you to be who you are." ~ Brené Brown, *Braving the Wilderness*, page 40.

SCRIPTURE

Do not conform to the pattern of this world, but be transformed by the renewing of the mind. ~ Romans 12:2

ACTION ITEM(S)

1. Start journaling – don't just sit and write, think about your intentions and your purpose before picking up your pen or pencil.
2. Your intentions should be to open the doors to the deepest parts of your soul.
3. Your purpose for writing should be to focus on you and your worries, fears, goals, dreams, and ultimate desires. "It's about discovering and giving voice to the secrets buried deep in your soul. It's about asking questions until you uncover the ones you've never asked." ~ Janet Conner, *Writing Down your Soul* (This is an excellent book to read to learn how to journal!)

"Most humans are never fully present in the now,
because unconsciously they believe that the next
moment must be more important than this one.
But then you miss your whole life, which
is never not now."

~ Eckhart Tolle

MASCULINE AND FEMININE ENERGY

INSPIRATION

I was watching a Tony Robbins video and I could actually see this woman who was very obviously in her masculine energy. It was incredibly inspiring... within 10-15 minutes of him talking with her, it almost looked like she melted back into her feminine energy. I spent a lot of time in masculine energy due to feeling rejected; one thing I was really good at was being independent and self reliant. If any man or woman tells you that they don't "need" anyone else, they are way too far into their masculine energy. If a man tells you that he hasn't cried in over 10 years, he needs to connect with his feminine energy. It is absolutely 100% normal for men to cry. If men cry as often as we women do, it might be time for them to reconnect with their masculine energy. The last thing a female wants is a man who cries more than she does.

Most of us suffer from wounds inflicted by our parents (unknowingly or now on their part). Healing these wounds is very important to the journey to becoming a perfect mixture of masculine and feminine energies. If you find yourself unable to connect with your feminine energy, which is often more creative, emotional, imaginative, intuitive, and soft, this is typically due to being rejected by your mother. There is also an abandonment wound; if one of your parents (or maybe even both) was either physically or emotionally not present, you might still be suffering from this wound. This causes low self worth, neediness, and being really clingy in a relationship. Sometimes this results in a woman who cannot help but tolerate a relationship with a married man. If you are wounded by a masculine energy, you will likely end up being controlling, aggressive, angry, and won't/can't cry.

SCRIPTURE

God created man in His own image, in the image of God He created him; male and female He created them. ~ Genesis 1:27

ACTION ITEM(S)

Answer the following questions

WOUNDED FEMININE TRAITS

Circle which traits you identify with:

- Victim
- Not owning your power
- Clingy
- Needy
- Attached
- Jealous
- Competitive
- Prone to comparison
- Manipulative
- Unconfident
- Weak (with no boundaries)
- Unable to say "No"
- Apologetic
- Vindictive
- Incapable of speaking up
- Verbose
- Co-dependent
- Desperate for love
- Self-sacrificing
- Drowned in emotions
- Restless

DIVINE FEMININE TRAITS

Circle which of these traits you identify with:

- Empowered
- Not afraid to speak up
- Strong boundaries
- Ask for what she needs
- Encourages other women
- Inspired
- Intuitive
- Compassionate
- Cooperative
- Collaborative
- Worthy
- Receptive
- Enjoys process of creation
- Embraces and accepts the body
- Authentic

Being aware of these traits is so very important. Create some action steps that you can take on a daily or weekly basis to check off the wounded list and move to the divine list. Men and women can have some from both of these lists. We want to achieve a mixture of divine feminine (way of the heart) and divine masculine traits (way of the mind). Traits provided by Dr. Falak Shaiikh from *The Soulmate Mantra* page 88.

"When there is balance and union of the feminine and the masculine within, the same is manifested in your reality as a union with your soulmate."

~ Dr. Falak Shaiikh

WOUNDED MASCULINE TRAITS

Circle which of these traits you relate to:

- Controlling
- Dominating
- Aggressive
- Abusive
- Unemotional
- Cold
- Distant
- Detached from emotion
- Prone to self-numbing (with porn, money, alcohol, or drugs)
- Stubborn
- Need to be right
- Critical
- Judgemental

DIVINE MASCULINE TRAITS

Circle which of these traits you relate to:

- Present
- Responsible
- Holds space
- Humble
- Honest
- Loyal
- Focused
- Disciplined
- Protective
- Supportive
- Encouraging
- Honors the feminine
- Emotionally available
- Powerful

NEGATIVE

INSPIRATION

"If the brain can get worse by constantly focusing on the problem then the brain can get better by understanding how to eliminate and replace the problem." ~ Caroline Leaf, *Switch on Your Brain*, page 61.

"If you focus on what is missing you can't sustain happiness."
~ Tony Robbins

Love is the greatest power in the universe. Make sure that you are making your decisions out of love. Make sure that when you are talking with people you are keeping your conversations positive and you are talking positively about other people. Eventually this will rub off on the other people with whom you surround yourself.

My mom always tries to talk with me about the news and I shut her down nearly every time. The news can be a very negative resource. My suggestion is to read the news in a Google feed just to stay up to date. I would also do research as to the things you should vote on, but besides that I definitely wouldn't watch it on a daily basis. They are only telling us what they want us to hear, and most often it is not both sides of the story.

The more you can keep the positive aspects of your life alive, the better off you will be. It is really easy to fall into a negative mindset. Unfortunately I think it is easier to fall into negativity than it is to stay positive in the world we live in. There is an abundance of everything you could ever want in life including money, love, success, joy, and happiness. If you are focusing on the negative in any situation you will get back out what you put in. Don't let your negative thoughts be an echo and come back to you with negative effects. Let your positive thoughts echo back to you an abundance of love, money, success, joy, and utter happiness.

SCRIPTURE

Therefore we do not lose heart. Even though our outward man is perishing, yet the inward man is being renewed day by day. For our light affliction, which is but for a moment, is working for us a far more exceeding and eternal weight of glory, while we do not look at the things which are seen, but at the things which are not seen. For the things which are seen are temporary, but the things which are not seen are eternal. ~ 2 Corinthians 4:16-18

ACTION ITEM(S)

1. Turn every situation in your daily life into something positive. I had the realization the other night that I don't **have** to take my kids to three different schools and pick them up from three different schools. **I get to.** My parents were never able to pick me up from school. It is extra time that I get to spend with them. I better take advantage of this while I can. Saying "I get to" in every situation that you usually say "I have to" will dramatically change your perspective on turning negatives into positives. What do you get to do today?
2. Make the choice to make even your worst days be your best days. Do this by writing down five things that happened today that you loved.

OVERWHELMED

INSPIRATION

This is extremely hard for me to admit, but this is my emotional "home." If I am ever going to feel a certain way, this is where my subconscious feels most comfortable. Sometimes I can get overwhelmed with everything I need to do and I end up doing nothing. This doesn't happen very often anymore, because I make a list and start crossing things off of that list. Every time a task gets marked off I am pretty sure my brain releases a little squirt of dopamine. I can promise you that if you are feeling overwhelmed and you skip a workout, meditation, or even five minutes of breathwork, the whole rest of your day will suffer. I have also learned that seeking a balance in life is always going to mean something different. One day it might be an hour long workout, work for seven hours, pick up kids from school, cook dinner, and get to bed at 10 pm; the next day it might mean work for five hours, go to the orthodontist, pick a sick kid up from school, work two more hours, and get in bed at 11 pm. It is all ok. You can't be too hard on yourself if you don't get a workout in one day or even take a break when you have too much going on.

I just finished the basement in my house pretty much by myself. I spent hours down there turning it from a cement slab into a beautiful, living space. I decided that until the basement was done I was not also going to bust my butt to get to the gym. Yes, it so happened to be physical labor, but it isn't like I was actually lifting weights and doing cardio. There was no way I was going to be so hard on myself to expect after getting up and down to lay the flooring that I would go to the gym. I could barely move after a few hours in the basement doing the trim or the flooring. Actually, I really don't know how people do that kind of work every day of their lives. Let's just say I took a couple of months off from working out.

SCRIPTURE

Trust in the Lord with all your heart, and do not lean on your own understanding. In all your ways acknowledge him, and he will make straight your paths. ~ Proverbs 3:5-6

ACTION ITEM(S)

1. Say no to things that don't excite you or bring you joy. No, I am not talking about taking out the trash. I am talking about when someone asks you to help them move. If it is someone you love then you will love helping them and it will bring you joy because you are doing it from the heart. If it is someone you barely know and you need some down time, SAY NO!
2. Make a daily schedule and stick to it. I use time chunking to keep me efficient. This is where I will mark myself off in increments of one to two hours depending on the task and make sure that I do it at the exact time I said I was going to. By exact I mean it happens 90% of the time. With three kids there are always things that pop up.
3. Wake up 30 minutes early to get a little more done that day.
4. Make sure you meditate to clear your mind of any nonsense that is going to distract you from the rest of your tasks. Someone once told me that if you can't meditate for 30 minutes then you should meditate for an hour. Let that one sink in. ;)

"A balanced life is a lie."

~ Gary Keller and Jay Papasan, *The One Thing*, page 73.

OVERWORKED

INSPIRATION

"I am overworked," every entrepreneur ever has said that at some point. I will say that having your own business is not for the faint of heart. At the same time you couldn't pay me enough to deal with rush hour and corporate America. I think that a lot of the reason we feel overworked is because we have to do things that we don't particularly like doing. I have learned to outsource the things that I don't like to do in my business. Whether that is my project manager or a virtual assistant, it helps me tremendously. I even have someone clean my house once a month. Even though you have to pick up so much to have someone come in and clean, it is absolutely worth coming home to a spotless house. When you are feeling overworked it is also because you are feeling out of balance. If, and I mean a huge IF, I ever worked a corporate job I would not be working more than 40 hours a week. Sometimes you have to set these boundaries and tell your boss that you get off of work at 5 pm every single day, no matter what. If you work for a decent company they will respect that.

I absolutely love what I do because I get to help entrepreneurs grow the brand/business of their dreams. It is almost as if I get to start a new business a few times a month. I would call this living vicariously through my clients.

SCRIPTURE

But they who wait for the Lord shall renew their strength; they shall mount up with wings like eagles; they shall run and not be weary; they shall walk and not faint. ~ Isaiah 40:31

ACTION ITEM(S)

1. Make a list of all of the tasks you do on a daily basis.
2. Make a list of the items that you could possibly outsource.
3. If you are unable to outsource at this time, try time blocking your schedule. Put your must dos on your schedule in hourly chunks to make sure these get done and then go in and time chunk the other things you need to do.

"You can't measure fulfillment with time. Fulfillment is what happens within and over time. It's how you show up. It's what you make of it. It's about being present, being intentional and releasing expectations."

~ Tara Renze, *Be Who You Came to Be*, page 46.

PEACEFUL

INSPIRATION

The three scenarios in which I feel the most peaceful are: at church, on the beach, and when I am meditating. Not everyone feels peaceful at church or with their own thoughts while meditating. Maybe your peace is in hiking in nature. One way to feel more at peace is by not paying attention to the inner critic inside you. Don't let your subconscious make up scenarios that just aren't true. If you can get to a point where you are at peace with yourself, then you are much closer to being at peace with others. I would spend as much time as you can with your peaceful thoughts. I have started taking baths – I light a candle, turn off the lights, and meditate. I wish I could spend more time on the beach listening to the waves crashing on the shore. On one of my trips to Cancun, the air conditioner in our room didn't work well, so I slept outside. I don't know if I have ever slept that well. So in this instance maybe having Alexa play crashing waves all night while you are sleeping would help you fall asleep and possibly even stay asleep.

SCRIPTURE

I have told you these things, so that in me you may have peace. In this world you will have trouble. But take Heart! I have overcome the world.
~ John 16:33

ACTION ITEM(S)

1. Write down all the things that bring you peace. It could be a person, a place, or an activity.
2. Start doing at least one of these things every single day, if not multiple times a day.

"There is no reason to get stressed-out. There is no reason for blowing up or shutting down. If you do not let this energy build up inside you, but be as fresh every moment as you would beo on a stress-free vacation. It is not life's events that are causing problems or stress. It is your resitance to life's events that is causing this experience."

~ Michael A. Singer, *The Untethered Soul: The Journey Beyond Yourself,* page 151

REGRETFUL

INSPIRATION

If you have regrets in life then that means a couple of things. You are living in the past and you haven't forgiven yourself. The hardest part about change is making a different choice than you made yesterday. I have gotten to a point in my life where I don't have any regrets. Some of the worst decisions I have ever made have proven to be the biggest learning lessons in life. This goes back to suffering from situations where you don't really have to suffer anymore. You can stop suffering from a situation anymore when you turn it into a positive learning lesson. To help you not have regrets, make sure you take action instead of fearing new things. I am sure you have heard the quote attributed to Lewis Caroll: , "In the end, we only regret the chances we didn't take, relationships we were afraid to have and the decisions we waited too long to make."

SCRIPTURE

Then when Judas, His (Jesus) betrayer, saw that Jesus was condemned, he changed his mind and brought back the thirty pieces of silver to the chief priests and the elders, saying, 'I have sinned by betraying innocent blood!' They said, 'What is that to us? See to it yourself.' And throwing down the pieces of silver into the temple, he departed, and he went and hanged himself. ~ Matthew 27:3-5

ACTION ITEM(S)

1. Get your regrets off of your chest. Write them out.
2. Go to the **FORGIVING** chapter and do the forgiveness practice for yourself.
3. Stop living in the past and realize everything happens for a reason and all you can do to change things is learn from what you did last time and take a different action next time.

"Always Do Your Best. Your best is going to change from moment to moment; it will be different when you are healthy as opposed to sick. Under any circumstance, simply do your best, and you will avoid self-judgment, self-abuse and regret."

~ Don Miguel Ruiz

RESENTFUL

INSPIRATION

Resentment can be very toxic and detrimental to any relationship. This lets the person who has disappointed you have control over you. The main thing is figuring out a way to let it go and try not to let it build up in the first place. One thing I have learned, in any relationship, is you should never withhold your feelings from a loved one. If you can explain to them how you feel without blaming or shaming them they can't argue with how you feel.

"Resentment is like drinking poison and then hoping it will kill your enemies." ~ Nelson Mandela

Think of the Holy Spirit inside of you created purely from love and then you have your ego that is for attack. Your spirit is going to be able to forgive and the ego will be attacking the person who you are feeling resentful towards. Let down that wall of pride and let the Holy Spirit take over. Ego is the great divide between our truth or our light and winning or our pride.

Turning pain into passion is going to be much better than it becoming fear, hatred, or resentment.

SCRIPTURE

And when you stand praying, if you hold anything against anyone, forgive them, so that your Father in heaven may forgive you your sins.
~ Mark 11:25

ACTION ITEM(S)

1. Pray to God this prayer "Dear God, I am willing to see ______ differently. Please let me see ______ through your eyes."

"Pain that is denied or ignored becomes fear or hate. Anger that is never transformed becomes resentment and bitterness."

~ Brené Brown, *Braving the Wilderness*, page 69.

SAD

INSPIRATION

I have spent plenty of time sad. I would say that in the long run I have been blessed with HOPE. There are very, very few times in my life when I have felt so sad that I just couldn't come out of it within a few hours or at most one day. It truly helps to always have something to look forward to. Right now in my life I envision myself with MY PERSON swinging on my porch swing and drinking wine, laughing, and having an amazingly deep conversation. If you are feeling sad for more than a couple of days and changing your physiology doesn't even help, please go to the **DEPRESSED** chapter.

Feeling sad is a normal emotion at times. It actually helps to just sit with it and just feel it. You just don't want sadness to become your emotional home. When sadness comes up, feel it, and then start thinking about things that you appreciate. If you have certain things that always make you sad when you think about them, see if you can change how you think about this situation. One thing that makes me sad everytime I think about it is being alone. I have changed this recently so I am free from my past and I am not tied down to someone I don't want to be with. I could keep being sad about this, or I can appreciate the fact that I am carefree and don't have to answer to anyone. You can imagine which one I'm choosing.

SCRIPTURE

The righteous cry out, and the Lord hears,
And delivers them out of all their troubles.
The Lord is near to those who have a broken heart,
And saves such as have a contrite spirit.
~ Psalm 34:17-18

For His anger is but for a moment,
His favor is for life;
Weeping may endure for a night,
But joy comes in the morning.
~ Psalm 30:5

ACTION ITEM(S)

1. Make a list of five things that always cheer you up.
2. Make a list of five things that you have to look forward to.
3. Make a list of the happiest moments in your life you have experienced so far.
4. Change your physiology – turn on your favorite song as loud as you can and just dance.

SAVED

INSPIRATION

If someone (the Bible) told you that if you prayed a particular prayer and followed Christ, that you could live for all eternity, would you do it? I did not grow up believing in being saved. I don't want religion to get in the way of this. It should be more about your relationship with God. I didn't grow up in a non-denominational church like I go to now. The church I go to preaches directly from the Bible and they don't waiver. There is an online campus, but if you happen to live in Kansas City, Missouri, I hope you will visit Abundant Life.

I didn't get saved at my church. I got saved at a church that I don't necessarily believe in everything they do. I grew up in a totally different religion. Yet, I still feel the Holy Spirit in all these places. This being said, it doesn't matter to me what religion you are and it shouldn't matter to anyone because it is ultimately your choice and your relationship with God. Some of the people closest to me in my life don't even believe in God at all. We still must love everyone where they are at right now. Do I pray for them to someday believe and pray this prayer? Of course! After all, I do want them to spend eternity with me in Heaven. This earth is a tiny glimpse of our lives, but you might as well make it the best it can be while you are here.

SCRIPTURE

That if you confess with your mouth the Lord Jesus and believe in your heart that God has raised Him from the dead, you will be saved. For with the heart one believes unto righteousness, and with the mouth confession is made unto salvation. ~ Romans 10:9-10

For whoever calls on the name of the Lord shall be saved.
~ Romans 10:13

ACTION ITEM(S)

1. If you haven't been saved, my suggestion would be to pray the prayer below. All God wants is for us to aknowledge and to follow Him.

Dear Lord Jesus, I know that I am a sinner, and I ask for Your forgiveness. I believe You died for my sins and rose from the dead. I turn from my sins and invite You to come into my heart and life. I want to trust and follow You as my Lord and Savior.

SCARED

INSPIRATION

Let me ask you... What is it that you are scared of? I am scared of my kids growing up and saying they didn't have a happy childhood. I know I'm not perfect, but I am making a point to end some generational patterns I inherited from my family. Most often when we are scared it is because of something that happened in our past to make us scared for what might happen in the future. If you are living in the present moment, there is nothing to be afraid of. After all, most things in this world you can't control anyway and really God has the ultimate control and what is supposed to happen will happen. Is it always going to be what you want to happen? No, of course not. God has a plan for each of us and all we can do is try to be the best human we can be on a daily basis. Are we going to sin? Absolutely. Are we forgiven? Absolutely. If you are scared of everything all of the time then you probably have things from the past that you need to deal with. For instance, if you are always scared of being late, it might stem from a parent being late to pick you up and it is still a trigger. One time I asked my ex husband to drop my daughter off at the orthodontist and I was going to pick her up after the appointment and take her to school. Well, "mother of the year" completely forgot to go pick her up. When they tried to call me I was in the shower. She had to sit and wait for me for about 15 minutes and this was traumatic for her. I've lived through much worse than waiting for 15 minutes, so for me it didn't seem that bad. In hindsight I realize I shouldn't have downplayed her feelings, because she still felt abandoned and that there was something more important to me than her. She will always be scared of being late because of this one scenario. Not that being early is a bad thing, but hopefully she doesn't get all worked up and stressed out about being late later in life.

SCRIPTURE

Fear not, for I am with you; be not dismayed, for I am your God. I will strengthen you, I will help you, I will uphold you with my righteous right hand. ~ Isaiah 41:10

For he has said, 'I will never leave you nor forsake you.' So we can confidently say, 'The Lord is my helper; I will not fear; what can man do to me?' ~ Hebrews 13:5b-6

ACTION ITEM(S)

1. Write down the things that scare you the most.
2. Can you place a time in your past that might have made you scared of these things?
3. Reflect on what it might take to release what you are scared of.

"Fear is to love as darkness is to light."

~ Marianne Williamson, A Return to Love, page 22.

SELF LOVE

INSPIRATION

I am writing this at age 39 and a half. I am just now finding out what self love truly is. I just finished with my alignment coach and she told me to take care of myself. She preached self care and I kind of brushed it off until the last of our sessions. Loving yourself means putting your oxygen mask on first on the airplane. You should use this in every aspect of your life and especially if you have children. If you are stressed, worried, anxious, and not fully present, guess who also suffers besides you? You should absolutely take the time to meditate, take a bath, read, journal, go out with friends, and so on. One of the most powerful moments of my life so far happened just last week. I took a bath and I did a self care meditation for women at the same time. I shut the lights off and just relaxed. It was absolutely amazing. If you aren't showing up for yourself you are never going to show up for someone else as your true self. God created you in his image so you would love your body, mind, and spirit. Keep this in mind when you are taking care of yourself.

How are you going to live an abundant life if you feel like you aren't enough and you don't deserve it? There are plenty of people out there who I don't necessarily feel like they deserve the abundance of money they have, but they have in most cases earned it. This also doesn't mean that they are happy with themselves. We all know that having money and fame doesn't make you happy. I feel like living a life on purpose is what gives us hope, love, and success.

SCRIPTURE

Though a host should encamp against me, my heart shall not fear: though war should rise against me, in this will I be confident.

~ Psalm 27:3

ACTION ITEM(S)

1. Create a daily self care ritual or multiple daily self care rituals here are some ideas also inspired by Rachel Watkins in her course **Restoring Harmony.** Plan out your entire month with these ideas.
    - Take a bath
    - Journal
    - Write down 10 things you are grateful for about yourself
    - Write yourself an encouragement note
    - Journal about your favorite memory
    - Read your astrology chart
    - Take a bike ride
    - Get out in nature and just walk
    - Order in dinner
    - Read some inspirational quotes, maybe even write your own
    - Volunteer somewhere
    - Light candles and sit in silence
    - Go shop around your local bookstore
    - Go to the movies by yourself
    - Get yourself some flowers
    - Go get a manicure or pedicure
    - Sing really loudly to your favorite song in the car
    - Dance in your kitchen while you are making yourself a healthy snack or meal
    - Create a vision board
    - Listen to a new podcast
    - Write a review for a business you visited
    - Pay for someone's coffee at your local coffee shop
    - Go get a massage
    - Do yoga
    - Take a nap
    - Smile at every stranger you see
    - Watch the sunset in silence
    - Read a book
    - Take a night to stargaze
    - Donate to your favorite charity

2. The more you take care of yourself, the more you are going to truly see, appreciate, and value yourself. It is amazing how taking a bath, meditating, breathwork, and valuing your quiet time can prove to yourself how valuable you are. Another thing about this is that your kids, if you have them, will see this and see how important it is and then they will take this trait with them and become an adult who practices self love and self care.

*"Tell yourself, 'I love you' on a daily basis.
I mean, why not? I told my dog
I loved him 22 times a day, so why
can't I say it to myself once?"*

~ Gina Giro, Self Love School

STRESSED

INSPIRATION

"Reaction is the key word here. You cannot control the events or circumstances of your life, but you can control your reactions. And controlling those reactions is the difference between healthy minds and bodies and sick minds and bodies." ~ Dr. Caroline Leaf, *Switch on your Brain*, page 37.

A study by the American Medical Association found that stress is a factor in 75% of all illnesses and diseases that people suffer from today.

I can tell you that being a single parent with three kids and owning my own business is stressful at times to say the least. I am solely responsible for their wellbeing, food on the table, and where my next job is coming from. I don't know what's going on at their fathers' houses, but I do know that I am solely responsible for ensuring that they know their mom loves them unconditionally. I have been blessed in this aspect and I know that my kids are very well taken care of at their fathers' house. Unless there is abuse happening that you can prove there isn't much that you can do about what happens at the other parent's house. Stressing about it isn't going to help.

Stress can mean so many different things for so many people. It might be studying for a college exam; maybe you wouldn't be so stressed if you hadn't waited until the last minute to study. We can help ourselves not get so stressed out if we would be proactive in situations versus reactive. You don't want stress to be your emotional home that you keep going back to. I am convinced that stress can cause your body to start attacking itself in every way.

SCRIPTURE

For I, the Lord your God, will hold your right hand, Saying to you, 'Fear not, I will help you.' ~ Isaiah 41:13

These things I have spoken to you, that in Me you may have peace. In the world you will have tribulation; but be of good cheer, I have overcome the world. ~ John 16:33

ACTION ITEM(S)

1. Meditation can rewire new circuits in the brain. If you even just start out with five minutes a day and move up to 10 the next week. 20 minute meditations happen to be perfect for me. You can determine what number works for you, but meditation (and breath work while you are meditating) will rejuvenate your mind.

STRUGGLING IN AN INTIMATE RELATIONSHIP

INSPIRATION

I do believe that until we have healed from our past, we will be challenged with the partners we choose to help us heal. God puts people in your life that will help you work through emotional triggers. He truly wants us to be happy and become our true selves.

Often I wonder why we continue to end up in the same kind of situation, but with a different person. Hence why second marriage divorce rates are even higher than first. If you are feeling like you want more out of your relationship, my first advice would be to read or listen to *The Seven Levels of Intimacy* by Mathew Kelly. This book is amazing and I would say that if your partner is willing to read it with you, your relationship will make leaps and bounds going forward. If your partner won't read this book with you or take any of the steps outlined to move forward, my biggest piece of advice is you become who you want your partner to be and pray that they follow suit. Most people who notice a positive difference in you will start to realize that they need to step up their game also. The following list comes from Kelly's book. It might not make much sense out of the context of the book, but take my word for it, it is the best book I have read on creating more intimacy in your relationship.

Level #1: Clichés. This is the type of relationship that tends to be surface level. You should be moving from small talk to talking about your dreams and deepest desires.

Level #2: Facts. This is the type of intimacy that if you are sharing facts and not feelings then you are missing out. You don't want to hide behind facts and just tell someone exactly what happened in your day. You want to feel comfortable expressing how the situations made you feel. When you stick with facts you are staying at a surface level.

Level #3: Opinions. The best way to deal with opinions is to listen and take into consideration that everyone is different. Being able to do this is a really great sign of self awareness. The point here is to not be narrow minded.

Level #4: Hopes and Dreams. "Our dreams are the vision that shapes our lives, and the vision that shapes our relationships." (page 175). You should definitely be able to share your hopes, goals, and dreams with your partner.

Level #5: Feelings. The key here is vulnerability. "Sometimes it is very healthy just to accept our feelings for what they are, rather than analyzing them endlessly. Feelings don't always need a reason." (page 194). Listen to your partner and you will get to know how people feel and why they feel that way.

Level #6: Fears, Faults, and Failures. This is the emotional equivalent of nakedness. Learn to walk bravely with your partner and not try to fix or judge them.

Level #7: Legitimate Needs. The key here is to not focus on illegitimate wants and focus primarily on the legitimate needs. Relationships aren't always about getting what you want, it is about becoming the best version of yourself.

SCRIPTURE

Therefore a man shall leave his father and his mother and hold fast to his wife, and they shall become one flesh. ~ Genesis 2:24

ACTION ITEM(S)

1. Read this to your significant other:
   "In fact, we were brought together for healing purposes. There will be something in your personality which is bound to trigger the unhealed parts of me, and I will trigger yours. But we can see this relationship differently. Through the grace of God, it can become a healing

environment rather than an emotional torture chamber.

Then I think I can work on those parts of myself, and you can work on those parts of you. We can even grow beyond these things. I just need you to know that I'm trying. Please share with me, but try not to attack or judge me for these wounds I carry. And I will try my best to do the same for you. Then holiness will be served here, and the relationship can deepen. Forgive me if you can, and I vow to try to forgive you." ~ Marianne Williamson, *Enchanted Love*, page 32.

2. Practice what you preach and start taking action to become your true self and show that to your partner. If they are the one for you, they will start to follow your lead.
3. Set up a date night to talk about your hopes, goals, and dreams. If you are single, write them down in your journal.

"Do what you did at the beginning of a relationship and there won't be an end."

~ Tony Robbins

"When you begin to heal your old wounds, your wellness improves mentally, physically, emotionally, and spirituality. Your soul will begin to radiate a light from within giving you a path of self discovery, self love and self worth to live your life full of strength and vitality."

~ Alicia Zeller, Finding Radiance

STUCK

INSPIRATION

"You will think the same thoughts and then make the same choices that lead to the same behaviors that create the same experiences that produce the same emotions. Over time, you've created a set of hardwired neurological networks in the brain and you have emotionally conditioned your body to live in the past and that past becomes your future." ~ Dr. Joe Dispenza, *Becoming Supernatural*, page 31.

There are many moments in my life I can look back on and see I was doing exactly this. Our brains literally don't know the difference between what is really currently happening and a thought of a past memory that triggers an emotion. Our brains think that it is happening over again even though the situation isn't even currently happening. This is another great way to get stuck in those past emotions. If you are in a certain emotional state most of the time, my suggestion is to find a way to get out of it. That is one of the main purposes of this book. If you are typically in a positive emotion, by all means stay there!

In the past the two emotions that I've been most comfortable in are overwhelm and guilt. As a mom this is probably pretty common especially with little kids and working. I also know men carry a lot of overwhelm and guilt when it comes to taking care of their house financially.

SCRIPTURE

Do not remember the former things,
Nor consider the things of old.
Behold, I will do a new thing,
Now it shall spring forth;
Shall you not know it?
I will even make a road in the wilderness
And rivers in the desert. ~ Isaiah 43:18-19

I know how to be abased, and I know how to abound. Everywhere and in all things I have learned both to be full and to be hungry, both to abound and to suffer need. I can do all things through Christ who strengthens me. ~ Philippians 4:12-13

ACTION ITEM(S)

1. Modeling - find someone you look up to and do what they do. Eat what they eat, read what they read, start the healthy habits that they have, do the things they do. Find out as much as you can about them without being weird.
2. Make a list of the things that make you feel free. Come up with at least five.

SUICIDAL

Chapter by Jeremy Wood

INSPIRATION

As you descend the lights in your life dim, hopelessness sinks in and eventually you're asking extremely dangerous questions about life and whether you want to be a part of it. The scariest aspect of the whole ordeal is how easily it can set in.

Maybe you've never experienced thoughts of suicide, or just giving up – if you haven't, stay alert! Learn to recognize the feelings that can lead to those thoughts, and when you sense them get help, talk, communicate, do something. Don't continue to dig!

Depression can come from chemical imbalances or deficiencies in your brain, but in my own experiences it can also come from just staying in a hole. Instead of trying to get out you stay there, digging deeper and deeper, until not going on actually begins to sound reasonable. Your situation seems so hopeless, that the default position at that point is to just stop... everything.

My own personal experience comes from a period of about 18 months that was marked by many difficult situations. Five beloved family members (a cousin, grandfather, two uncles, and an aunt) died; my business was in real danger of failing (thereby erasing all of the time and money I had invested into it), which led to me splitting with my business partner (who was my best friend at the time) soon after I had taken over the business, I discovered that my former partner and friend had defaulted on a loan (which I didn't know about) that was taken out in the business' name]. Further, my personal health was not good, and for the first time in my life I had to have surgery – not once, but three times, along with three trips to the emergency room. For me, that was the worst period of my life. Every time I turned around it felt as though something was going wrong – and not just the normal trivial things (though those seemed to be pecking away at me as well), but big things. Death on a large scale, my business was on life support, losing a friend and partner – along with the sense of betrayal I felt from his actions, poor health (and the enormous costs of paying for that health), along with the tremendous sense of failure I felt about who I should be for my wife and children.

After things finally seemed to be leveling out – my wife and I, along with our two young boys, went to my favorite place on Earth – the Rocky Mountains. I thought I could recharge there, or at least get my mind straightened out. What happened instead was just more problems and coming to the awful realization that I was just done. The mountains meant nothing, the fresh air didn't seem to hit my lungs, and I didn't enjoy being with those I loved the most. My wife, who unbeknownst to me was noticing all of this, finally asked me what was wrong. Honestly, I didn't have an answer at that point. I felt like a spaceship completely adrift in an asteroid field, with all my shields depleted (yes, I'm a Star Wars fan). I can honestly say I never really considered just ending things for myself, but I also wouldn't have minded if a huge rock just hit the ship and ended it for me. I remember thinking I don't WANT to die, but if it happened, I'd be okay with that. More time passed, and more people began to notice – even people who didn't really know me. My Dad asked me one time what was wrong. I told him I was fine. He told me he knew better, and that whatever it was, he could see it all over me.

I won't say my family did an intervention, but my wife, parents, and a couple of friends basically forced me to get help in the form of going to a doctor. I'd set appointments and skip them, and then finally my wife decided she was going to go with me – even the Doctor said, "Okay, you can take the handcuffs off of him," when I arrived with her by my side. I spoke with him for a while, explained everything, and then they ran a battery of tests on me, and eventually prescribed medication to take, as a chemical called Serotonin in my brain was low.

I was extremely ashamed (and still am a little embarrassed) to have to take a stupid little pill to even things out for me. The doctor told me that if I had broken my arm, I'd come to him, and this was no different. It was to me, though, as I knew people like my dad and grandfathers who had fought in wars, who seemed fine – and here I was needing medication for a bad year or so? What I didn't know was that they, along with a lot of other people I would have never guessed, also needed help. It still didn't take the stigma away in my mind, but it helped.

The TV commercials seemed to show that you take your little pill, and everything in the world just suddenly becomes great again, but for me that didn't happen. I will admit the valleys in my life didn't seem to go as deep anymore, as in my earlier state, when even a small thing would knock me down pretty easily, but I didn't feel well. I had better focus, or perspective, when things didn't go well for me, but I wasn't right. Something was still wrong... So I looked to God.

In my life, I had always been one to turn from God when things got rough. I was always a person who would say, "Fine. You don't wanna help me, I'll do it myself." At times, I'd come back begging for help, but it never really felt like I was in a situation I couldn't get myself out of. This time was different. I felt so battered, so broken, and so worn out, I really did just offer myself up to Him. And as you might imagine, He showed up. It would take a whole book to explain what He did for me, but I'm here to tell you when you seek God with your whole heart He makes Himself known (Jeremiah 29:13). So, with the help of my wife, family, and friends, that's what I did.

The following is a process that came about from the teachings of three great men of God: Dr. George Westlake (former Pastor of Sheffield Family Life Center in Kansas City, Missouri), Pastor Peter Nugent (former Pastor of Grace Baptist Church in Lee's Summit, Missouri), and Pastor Phil Hopper (Abundant Life Church in Lee's Summit, Missouri). These men spent time with me, talked to me, emailed me, preached to me, and showed me a way out of the feeling of despair and worthlessness that permeated my being. They showed me that I was worth so much to God, that He sent His son Jesus Christ to die for me so that He could spend eternity with me. As Pastor Westlake often said, "He knows everything about me and died for me anyway and would have done so even if I was the only person who ever needed it."

If any of the things you've read from my story seem familiar, or you find yourself in the position I was in – or worse – let me encourage you to try the process that God and I go through to shatter the darkness and bring back the light in my life. It takes time, patience, a lot of practice, and faith, but, trust me, when you go looking for God, you'll find He has been there waiting for you all along! That the Creator of the Universe loves us that much is incomprehensible to me. You will find your self worth in Him, and that is where you will find the ultimate peace.

SCRIPTURE

Fear not, for I am with you; Be not dismayed, for I am your God. I will strengthen you, Yes, I will help you, I will uphold you with My righteous right hand. ~ Isaiah 41:10

Whoever sheds man's blood, By man his blood shall be shed; For in the image of God He made man. ~ Genesis 9:6

But his delight is in the law of the LORD; and in his law doth he meditate day and night. ~ Psalm 1:2

Be careful for nothing; but in every thing by prayer and supplication with thanksgiving let your requests be made known unto God.And the peace of God, which passeth all understanding, shall keep your hearts and minds through Christ Jesus.Finally, brethren, whatsoever things are true, whatsoever things are honest, whatsoever things are just, whatsoever things are pure, whatsoever things are lovely, whatsoever things are of good report; if there be any virtue, and if there be any praise, think on these things. Those things, which ye have both learned, and received, and heard, and seen in me, do: and the God of peace shall be with you. ~ Philippians 4:6-9

ACTION ITEM(S)

1. Make a list... Write out whatever is Honest, Just, Pure, Lovely, of Good Report, Virtuous . anything worthy of praise in your life – and DWELL on those things! Get away from whatever or whoever is causing your stress, anxiety, depression, or thoughts of darkness – and clear your mind – so you can simply focus on the things that make up your list.
2. Really get into the word of God. My suggestion is start in the New Testament, then read the Old Testament afterward. In addition, Proverbs (being a book of wisdom) has 31 chapters – so read the chapter that corresponds to the date. If it's the 10th of the month, then read the 10th chapter! The other books of wisdom are fantastic to read as well when you're just looking for direction in your life.

"Suicide does not end the chances of life getting worse, suicide eliminates the possibility of it ever getting better."

~ Kat Calhoun

TRIGGERED

INSPIRATION

Tony Robbins says that people have two different internal beliefs :

1. We are scared that we aren't enough.
2. We are scared we won't be loved.

I have definitely come to find out that my triggers of the fear of not being enough happen when someone chooses something or someone over me. It could be breaking plans or drinking too much. I am also triggered big time when anyone questions how good of a mom I am. I think at times we all question our parenting. We are all parenting for the first time at some point. Even if you had amazing parents it is soooo different when it is your kids and you are 100% responsible for them. One of my best accomplishments in life so far is being a mom. I just want my kids to grow up and say that they were happy and loved. I would say this is true so far.

Even the best of relationships are going to trigger us. We have to be very clear to our partner what causes our triggers and be curious about theirs. If you have that laid out on the table maybe you can avoid a few fights in the duration of your relationship. If you do get triggered then I would take a step back and become self aware. I have been in a couple of relationships where I had done something to trigger the other person and they started saying mean, terrible things to me. My suggestion is to definitely not take these things to heart, because hurt people hurt people. On the other hand I also know the kinds of things that my exes said to me were absolutely not ok. The person who is going to be my person for life will never say mean and terrible things to me no matter how mad they are. Also, actions speak louder than words so if possible take a minute to chill when you are triggered and do your best to realize that this situation is completely different than the situation that originally happened to create this emotion.

"This chain of training from human to human, from generation to generation, is perfectly normal in human society. You don't need to blame your parents for teaching you to be like them. What else could they teach you but what they know? They did the best they could, and if they abused you, it was due to their own domestication, their own fears, their own beliefs. They had no control over the programming they received, so they couldn't have behaved any differently." ~ Don Miguel Ruiz, *The Four Agreements*, page 96.

SCRIPTURE

Now may the Lord of peace Himself give you peace always in every way. The Lord be with you all. ~ II Thessalonians 3:16

ACTION ITEM(S)

Journal and ask yourself these questions:

1. What triggers fear in me? Anger? Frustration? Depression?
2. Is fear triggered by my environment and/or relationships, or is it inside of me?
3. Where does it come from? When did I first experience this trigger?
4. How can I recognize the trigger? Where does it start in my body?
5. How do I react to it?
6. How can I become conscious of this trigger so it doesn't have dominion over me?
7. When it comes again, how can I recognize it and what can I do differently?
8. If you are upset just melt into it and by this I mean just let your body flop in every way – if you have to sit down, do it. When you relax all of your muscles it helps all of that tension that happens when you get triggered.

UGLY AND OVERWEIGHT

INSPIRATION

Let's be honest, at some point in time each of us has felt ugly. Whether it was just a bad hair day or a bad hair week. Sometimes pictures make us look better than the mirror and sometimes worse. For myself I would say that I do not take good pictures at all. I have just never been photogenic. I often ask myself and even others (no for real) is that really what I look like?! I have come to appreciate some of the things I used to not like about myself, my face shape for one. I saw an actress the other day with my same face shape and she was beautiful and it helped me appreciate my looks. God made you exactly the way you were supposed to be made and I think a lot of times we compare ourselves too often to others. I am 100% guilty of this. It comes from insecurities about ourselves from the past. If you can learn to appreciate others for their beauty or handsomeness then you will be a lot better off in the long run. And also trust that God you are beautiful.

With most Americans being overweight, this is a tough one. Learning to appreciate your body's a huge task. Even the most beautiful and fit people still have issues with their body. Overcoming these insecurities and appreciating how your body moves and what you like to do for fitness is key. Somehow with all of the energy healing and self love and care that I have been doing lately, I suddenly started to just drop weight. Yes, I have been working out and eating better, but it seems easy this time. If you can make it a lifestyle and change your relationship with food the same will likely happen for you. Food is for us to survive and thrive, not for stress eating or for fun. Don't get me wrong, I love nothing more than going to dinner with family and friends and even having a glass of wine. I have gotten to the point where I only eat until I am slightly full and it is working. This is the only body you get so you should most definitely take care of it. Every year the average age of death is increasing; if you want to feel good into your 90s, exercise and eating right are key. Find an exercise that you love to do. I personally love dancing, TRX, and classes more than I like just going to the gym and lifting weights and the stinkin' treadmill or elliptical. Remember nutrition is 80% of the battle. I think most people know what they should and shouldn't be eating. I personally believe that we need a small amount of carbs in our diet to keep our energy levels up. That being said, I am not talking about candy bars and cinnamon rolls. I am saying that having rice with veggies and some protein is a perfect meal to fuel your body.

After all God made You, You. Perfectly, You.

SCRIPTURE

Your beauty should not come from outward adornment, such as elaborate hairstyles and the wearing of gold jewelry or fine clothes. Rather, it should be that of your inner self, the unfading beauty of a gentle and quiet spirit, which is of great worth in God's sight.

~ 1 Peter 3:3-4

ACTION ITEM(S)

1. Write down three things that you really appreciate about your appearance.
2. Tape them on your mirror and say them every morning.
3. Mel Robbins gives herself a high five every time she walks by a mirror. Just try it. It is kind of funny. I always say "You go girl" when I do it.
4. Write down all of the negative thoughts that come from your inner critic. Cross them out and replace them with positive thoughts.

UNFAITFUL

Chapter by Liesl Hays

INSPIRATION

I think many of us assume affairs happen in a moment of overwhelming passion. We get totally swept up and it just happens. While I'm confident some affairs start this way, I believe most don't. In reality, infidelity usually occurs in small seemingly insignificant moments that eventually become extremely significant.

Affairs often begin with little betrayals that fill a need. They start with exchanged phone numbers to discuss work related topics and eventually transition into personal exchanges. Infidelity happens through the subtle attraction that lingers in your mind about someone else. Instead of putting it away, you decide to nurse it little by little. After a series of these events, you start to realize you're dressing up for work everyday and working out like you're 22 again; but not for you – for them. Then one day you realize the person you go to when you're feeling down is no longer your spouse.

Affairs happen because of a series of tiny moments. Tiny moments that become big moments. What tiny moments are pulling you away from your spouse?

SCRIPTURE

Truthful words stand the test of time, but lies are soon exposed.
~ Proverbs 12:19

People with integrity walk safely, but those who follow crooked paths will slip and fall. ~ Proverbs 10:9

ACTION ITEM(S)

Perhaps you're reading this because you're thinking about having an affair. Or, it's possible you've already emotionally or physically abandoned your spouse for someone else. Wherever you are, I want you to know that it isn't too late to begin making things right. Here are some things that helped me:

1. Become honest and forgive yourself: It's time to accept the truth of your story. It might not be pretty. Your infidelity isn't easy to accept. Undoubtedly you've hurt a lot of people along the way. There were plenty of lies, deceitful behavior, and stories you'd prefer never to talk about. It's time to be brutally honest with yourself. Accept the truth of your story. Forgiveness is waiting on the other side of this. Until you can come clean with yourself, you won't be able to make amends with the people you love. Give yourself time and space to process the choices you've made. There is beauty on the other side of this mistake, but you must start by accepting it as such.
2. Uncover the root: One of the first things my therapist asked me post-affair was: Why did you have an affair? At the time, I had never explored the answer to this question. Most of the time infidelity happens because of something deeper you need to address in yourself. Perhaps love was modeled to you backwards and you are constantly picking people to date who aren't good for you. Or, maybe you're afraid of true intimacy with your spouse so you unintentionally self-sabotage your relationship by cheating. Whatever your reasoning, it's important to uncover the root of your decision so you can actually address it.
3. Explore your relationship needs: One of the biggest mistakes we make in our romantic relationships is assuming one person can fulfill all our needs. We are deeply complicated people who need a circle of friends and our spouse to support us. Typically, we step out on our spouses because they aren't filling a need we have. We under-

estimate the value of platonic friendships to help cultivate our happiness.

For instance, my friend Maki is always there when I need someone to tell me the hard truth. My friend Melissa is always a positive and uplifting voice. Jodi is the person I come to when I want to be silly and care-free. Affairs are often rooted in a need that isn't being fulfilled in your current relationships (friends, family, or spouse). While your spouse cannot fulfill all your needs, it's important to find a group of people who can fill the gaps.

Start by creating a list of your unique needs. Then, inventory the people in your life who are meeting each area. If you have gaps, maybe it's time to ask that neighborhood mom out for coffee.

"Your path is just as important as everyone else's.

The life you don't want has significant meaning.
It is here to wake you up and remind you of what actually matters.

Your quiet brokenness is preparing you for something beautiful.

Just wait."

~ Liesl Hays

UNFORGIVING

INSPIRATION

“In the special relationship, we are always trying to hide our weaknesses. In the holy relationship, it’s understood that we all have unhealed places, and that healing is the purpose of our being with another person. We don’t try to hide our weaknesses, but rather we understand that the relationship is a context for healing through mutual forgiveness.“
~ Marianne Williamson, *A Return to Love,* page 115.

“This brings us to one of the most difficult topics for the human psyche and spirit. Learning to forgive those who have wronged us is very , very difficult for most of us. But the ideas that we have just discussed can help to liberate us from the destructive spirit of unforgiveness.”
~ Matthew Kelly, *Seven Levels of Intimacy,* page 210.

I would like to add to this and say that this is one area of my life I have been greatly challenged in up until the last few years. I was able to forgive the people in my life who didn’t love me the way I needed to be or should have been loved as a child. I honestly do believe that we are put through trials and traumas in order to become strong adults who like to help others through tough times. There is one person in my life in particular who I worked very hard at forgiving. It so happens to be my ex husband (my son’s father). Through God’s grace for both of us are in a really good place right now. The main thing to remember in forgiving situations is people don’t necessarily do things TO you. They create actions that are positive or negative and you allow them to affect you, which can create suffering in your life. Don’t give anyone the power and fall victim, saying that someone did something to you. More often than not whatever they have done is because of their own negative issues and it isn’t even about you at all.

SCRIPTURE

And be kind to one another, tenderhearted, forgiving one another, even as God in Christ forgave you. ~ Ephesians 4:32

Bearing with one another, and forgiving one another, if anyone has a complaint against another; even as Christ forgave you, so you also must do. ~ Colossians 3:13

ACTION ITEM(S)

1. Make a list of people who you need to forgive.
2. Try to understand why they made the actions they made.
3. Be vulnerable with them and talk through your struggles.
4. Read the **FORGIVING** chapter and then do the action items.

UNGRATEFUL

INSPIRATION

Anytime you are focusing on the negative, you are being ungrateful. We are in an age where we think we deserve everything without having to work for it. We call this entitlement. I have definitely looked at my children in the last few years and thought, "why in the world do you think that you deserve for me to pay you for chores or pay your cell phone bill when you didn't even hold up your end of the bargain and spend 10 minutes doing the dishes?" I think one of the things that I have realized as I have gotten older is that if you start to appreciate the little things in life you will feel ungrateful a lot less often. The sunrises and sunsets have either gotten more beautiful in the last year or I am truly learning how to appreciate this amazing creation of a planet. The more you can practice appreciation and gratitude and really truly feeling it you will probably find yourself being ungrateful almost never. In a relationship it is really easy to become ungrateful as we take so much for granted. If you wrote two things that you are grateful for every day for each person who lives in your house, you are going to be way less likely to take the people who you love the very most for granted.

SCRIPTURE

The Spirit of the Lord God is upon Me, Because the Lord has anointed Me To preach good tidings to the poor; He has sent Me to heal the brokenhearted, To proclaim liberty to the captives, And the opening of the prison to those who are bound. ~ Isaiah 61:1

ACTION ITEM(S)

1. List the top five happiest moments of your life so far. Make sure to write I am grateful for...
2. List your favorite place to vacation and write down all of the details you love. When you have done that, picture yourself there again in

the next year doing all of your favorite things.

3. Meditate on that for three to five minutes.
4. Add it to your vision board when you are done.

"Ungrateful people breed negativity. No one gets any pleasure from giving to an ungrateful person. When you show appreciation, the object of your attention blossoms and flourishes."

~ Paul McCabe

UNHEALTHY

INSPIRATION

Making a decision to be healthier can be changing one small thing every day or every week. If you are feeling like you need to make a change, just do it. Don't wait for Monday or the New Year. We can start making new, healthier habits at any point in time. What you eat is 80-90% of the problem. If you can get a handle on your nutrition then more than half of the battle is won. You have to get to the point where your mindset is eating to feed your body and not just eating out of boredom or some other emotion. Listen to your body. Most people know what they should and shouldn't be eating. I am not much for the fad diets, but I do take pieces of each one that I know work for my body.

In terms of working out, making a plan is the most important aspect here. Lifting weights if you are able to is the best way to lose fat. You are gaining muscle and when you are gaining muscle you are burning more calories all of the time. If you are only doing cardio and not lifting weights or at a minimum body weight exercises then you are burning the calories you are eating, but you aren't changing your body composition as far as fat and muscle.

This is all about mindset. Once I made losing the 15 pounds I gained during the Covid lockdown (and age is honestly just starting to catch up with me), an absolute must, those last few pounds came right off. If you make it a must and not just a should and you take positive action, then the weight starts to come off.

And remember we can't do everything on our own. Sometimes we do need a coach to hold us accountable, teach us new things, and keep us up on the latest health news.

SCRIPTURE

He makes the whole body fit together perfectly. As each part does its own special work, it helps the other parts grow, so that the whole body is healthy and growing and full of love. ~ Ephesians 4:16

ACTION ITEM(S)

1. List the things that make you feel healthy.
2. Write down a paragraph stating how you feel when you feel really good with lots of energy.
3. Watch TikTok videos on quick healthy recipes.
4. Plan out your meals and snacks for the week. If you have a plan then you are less likely to eat out or grab unhealthy snacks.
5. Create a workout plan. If you look on Pinterest or on YouTube you can find workouts for every level of fitness and even yoga all the way to weight training.
6. Stick to your plan. I promise a healthy lifestyle is going to pay off way longer than a quick diet and then going right back to your old ways.

UNLOVEABLE

INSPIRATION

The best way to start feeling loveable is to first forgive yourself and know that you are doing the best you can at this moment and move on. I realized at almost 40 years old that the reason I haven't been able to make a relationship work is because up until now I didn't know how to really take care of myself. I don't mean like I am not independent and can't take care of myself. I mean truly take care of myself. This includes meditation and taking time to actually be with just me and like it. Meditation has been the key for me to getting to a much more peaceful state of mind.

This can also include putting into practice daily self care routines. This idea came from my Alignment Coach. She told me in our last session working together that she thought this was the last piece to the puzzle for me to truly love myself so I would be able to find someone who could truly love me as me. I sure hope she is right! I always know that something is true and right when I get chills, and I had them on my knee caps when I was talking to her in this session. It was crazy powerful. If you knew that meditating for 15 minutes a day could absolutely change your life, would you do it?

SCRIPTURE

For God so loved the world that He gave His only begotten Son, that whoever believes in Him should not perish but have everlasting life.
~ John 3:16

But God demonstrates His own love toward us, in that while we were still sinners, Christ died for us. ~ Romans 5:8

He who does not love does not know God, for God is love. ~ 1 John 4:8

ACTION ITEM(S)

1. Write yourself a forgiveness letter.
2. Burn it.
3. Do a meditation for five minutes and repeat "I forgive you and I love you" (out loud or silently) for the entire five minutes.
4. Read the **SELF LOVE** chapter and do the action items.

UNSECURE

INSPIRATION

If your parents didn't establish a sense of security for you as a child you are more likely to crave security as an adult. Just remember as an adult you are going to be attracted to someone who is going to help you heal from childhood traumas. If you want to feel secure, make sure that you establish your boundaries early in a relationship.

"Our relationships, more than anything else, are the vehicles by which we try to understand the meanings of our childhoods." ~ Daphne Rose Kingma, *Coming Apart*, page 19.

If your partner is not giving you a sense of security then you probably need to sit down and have a conversation. The only way to feel really secure in a relationship is to know that your relationship is more intimate than a surface level. I've read Matthew Kelly's book *The Seven Levels of Intimacy* a few times. If you have a relationship that is intimate on each of these levels, how could you possibly not feel secure in a deep relationship like this? You can have some of these levels with other relationships in your life. It is so very important to feel secure in our relationships. If at a young age our parents didn't make us feel secure – the two most loving relationships we usually even know – we are probably always going to suffer from not feeling secure in most of our relationships as we get older.

SCRIPTURE

For I am persuaded that neither death nor life, nor angels nor principalities nor powers, nor things present nor things to come, nor height nor depth, nor any other created thing, shall be able to separate us from the love of God which is in Christ Jesus our Lord.

~ Romans 8:38-39

ACTION ITEM(S)

1. Write down the most secure relationships you have and why they make you feel secure.
2. Write down what is different about these relationships than the ones in which you don't feel so secure.
3. What can you do to offer more security in your relationships? If you become a secure person in your relationships this will help others follow your lead.

UNWANTED

INSPIRATION

Nobody wants to feel unwanted. I will tell you as a middle child this has to be the trending feeling amongst us. When I was little I would lay in the hallway under a blanket just so someone would step on me. Talk about needing some attention. We all want to feel loved and wanted. I am sure at some point in all of our lives we have felt a little unwanted. I know that my kids feel that way every single time they are talking to me and I am not listening. I know that someday they will understand and I also know that I need to be more present with everyone in my life. Nothing drives me more crazy than when I am talking to someone and they are on their phone or working. I am completely guilty of both of these. The best thing we can do as humans is realize our mistakes and quit repeating them so we never make others feel unwanted.

The main thing I will say with this chapter is getting to a point where you love yourself is powerful beyond measure. If you truly love and accept yourself there is no way that other people won't fall in love with you.

I have a dear friend who has a program called Self Love School. Her website is GinaGiro.com. It is such an awesome program and she is an amazing person. She is the one that told me how awesome Tony Robbins' Unleash the Power Within program would be – and it was life changing. Tony Robbins is the biggest inspiration in my life by far.

SCRIPTURE

Give thanks to the God of gods. His love endures forever. People will come and go, but God's love for you lasts for all time. ~ Isaiah 49:15–16

ACTION ITEM(S)

1. Write a list of your unique qualities.
2. Write a list of your positive qualities.

"Belonging is being somewhere you want to be, and they want you. Fitting in is being somewhere where you want to be, but they don't care one way or the other.

Belonging is being accepted for you. Fitting in is being accepted for being like everyone else.

If I get to be me, I belong. If I have to be like you, I fit in."

~ Brené Brown, *Braving the Wilderness*, page 160.

VULNERABLE

INSPIRATION

"I believe it comes about when we can be truly transparent, seeing the world clearly and letting the world see into us."
~ Roshi Joan Halifax

I was listening today to Dean Grazziosi and he was talking about the true person you are; the person you are when no one else is around. This is so true and I had never thought about this before. I realized that even today someone had asked me a question and I fibbed a little on the answer in an attempt to make myself look better. I guess this could be called a white lie. Even this shows true character and now that I am more aware of this moving forward I will change this habit and be 100% honest with others and myself. Also, if you listen to anyone who studies lying, they will tell you that 100% of people currently lie on a daily basis.

Vulnerability is one of the hardest aspects in life, but you will not have any of the deep loving relationships you desire if you aren't vulnerable. This takes letting your ego not be the ruler and becoming more open and expressing your true self to those you love. Being vulnerable takes tremendous courage and willpower. The hardest part for me has always been not to sink back into my habits of getting hurt and then putting my guard back up to protect myself so I don't get hurt again. In this situation the best advice is to not sink back into your old ways.

SCRIPTURE

We have spoken freely to you, Corinthians; our heart is wide open. You are not restricted by us, but you are restricted in your own affections. In return (I speak as to children) widen your hearts also.
~ 2 Corinthians 6:11-13

ACTION ITEM(S)

1. Ask for what you need.
2. Be willing to share your feelings.
3. Say what your intentions are and what you want.
4. Express what you really think and feel.
5. Be present and listen and then share.

"There can be no intimacy—emotional intimacy, spiritual intimacy, physical intimacy—without vulnerability. One of the reasons there is such an intimacy deficit today is because we don't know how to be vulnerable. It's about being honest with how we feel, about our fears, about what we need, and asking for what we need. Vulnerability is glue that holds intimate relationships together."

~ Brené Brown

WEAK

INSPIRATION

This is not an emotion I relate to a whole lot. At least not outwardly. I do feel like it has been very hard for me in life to admit the times when I've felt weak. The moments I have felt the most weak and powerless are when my heart was breaking and I had to power through, to keep working, and make sure my kids didn't see my weakness. Of course I want my girls and son to think of me as strong, safe, and secure. To me in this instance you should definitely reach out and ask for help. Asking for help is one of the hardest things in life to do. We can't do anything on our own all of the time. Hence why I asked some friends and family to write a chapter for this book. I knew some emotions needed to be addressed, but were ones I don't relate to all that well.

It is ok to show weakness at times. We can't be strong all of the time. I just had a chat tonight with a family friend who said, "Wow, I didn't realize you were struggling. You just seem to always have your shit together." I said, "Well, that is what I always wanted people to believe on the outside." He had no idea I was going to therapy, coaches, and many energy healers to work to heal from my past trauma. We have known each other for 15 years and he didn't know this about me until I recently started opening up and posting on Facebook and TikTok. My point in telling you all of this is that I see the benefit of realizing weakness and understanding the importance of asking for help or even letting people know I am struggling. It is ok and it will be ok. And me sharing might help them be ok.

SCRIPTURE

He gives power to the weak, And to those who have no might He increases strength. ~ Isaiah 40:29

ACTION ITEM(S)

1. Pray this prayer: *Have mercy on me, O Lord, for I am weak; O Lord, heal me, for my bones are troubled.* ~ Psalms 6:2
2. Stand for two minutes in a Wonder Woman or Captain America pose. It sounds dorky, but it is actually proven that you will have more confidence after doing it.

WHAT'S MY PURPOSE

INSPIRATION

It took me six years to finish this book. Some people might feel and know what their purpose is, yet don't know how to achieve it. The entire time I was writing this book it was so obvious that I was supposed to be doing this. I just finished reading The Seven Levels of Intimacy (again) by Matthew Kelley. Your purpose will always be aligned with being the best version of yourself and your ultimate purpose is to be the best version of yourself. I started crying when I read this passage. It was so powerful to realize that I am currently living out my purpose. Some days it just feels like it is closer than others. I ultimately know that I am on the right path.

I am so proud of you for even seeking this out. So many people stay completely oblivious as to how they can contribute to society. GO YOU!

One thing I would definitely say is figuring out what ignites your soul on fire. What is it that makes you tick? What is your why? What gets your heart racing in a good way? Often the thing we are really passionate about comes from a healing journey that we have been on. My passion is helping others work through their issues and ultimately heal and keep moving on their path to enlightenment. Another really great question to ask yourself is: what makes you unique from others? If you can figure out what sets you apart you can figure out how to value yourself in a unique way.

SCRIPTURE

For I know the plans I have for you, declares the Lord, plans for welfare and not for evil, to give you a future and a hope. ~ Jeremiah 29:11

The purpose in a man's heart is like deep water, but a man of understanding will draw it out. ~ Proverbs 20:5

ACTION ITEM(S)

1. Pray: "Dear God, how do I become the best version of myself. Please lead me in Your direction."
2. I guarantee that your ultimate purpose has something to do with a passion you have. Journal about everything you are passionate about. If it gets your heart racing and blood pumping, I bet it is likely a clue to your purpose.

"Our essential purpose is to become the-best-version-of-ourselves."

~ Matthew Kelly, *The Seven Levels of Intimacy*, page 36.

WORRIED

INSPIRATION

When you ask yourself, what are the things I worry about? Let me ask you is there anything you can actually do about them. Trying to have control over situations is not going to help you in the long run. The weirdest moment in my life as a mother so far is watching my daughter drive away for the first time when she turned 16. It made me realize that I need to give up the idea of having control over her life now. It was a scary and very proud moment and I worried like crazy until she came home. Then later that night she took my other daughter to church and I just watched them drive away and thought ok there is nothing I can do and I am not going to worry. I kind of let the worry hit me as they were driving away and then let it pass through me instead of letting it get stuck.

Did you know that worrying is a sin? Worrying means you do not trust that God will take care of everything for you. I understand that church isn't for everyone, but for me I find a sense of peace when sitting in church as I don't worry or stress about anything. If you pray about different situations in your life that you worry about and have absolutely no control over you will also feel a sense of peace. Worrying is the opposite of having faith. Don't let your worries scare you away from living your amazing future.

SCRIPTURE

Why worry about tomorrow? Your heavenly Father knows what you need. ~ Matthew 6:25-33

Do not be anxious about anything, but in everything by prayer and supplication with thanksgiving let your requests be made known to God. ~ Philippians 4:6

ACTION ITEM(S)

1. Pray for God to take your troubles away and make you feel at peace. Ultimately God's will will be done so no need to worry.
2. Write down the things that worry you the most. Are there some action steps you can take to make some of the worry go away?

"Worry is like a rocking chair: it gives you something to do, but it never gets you anywhere."

~ Erma Bombeck

MY STORY

I have been writing this story since I was a little girl. I would write with my little hands on pieces of lined white paper and throw them in the trash every time. I always wondered why anyone would want to read "my" story. Well here I am, age 39 and finally publishing my story to share with the world in hopes of helping even just one person love their journey.

My first memory was when I was about 6 years old and my mom found a roller bottle of perfume in my jewelry box. She knew I had earlier asked for one of those at the store and she had said no. This was not my last bout with stealing. I was lucky she didn't make me return it to the store, that would have been mortifying.

I am sure my mom grounded me. I was the middle child – all middle children can relate even if all oldest and youngest children roll their eyes. I find it so interesting that now I have a middle child and tell her all the time life is what you make it. If you want attention, go get it.

Ok rewind, one of my next memories is getting on an airplane to California to stay with my dad for the summer. It was a situation where I was completely torn to leave my mom and see my dad who I only got to see twice a year. Leaving my mom meant being scared of what might happen to her while I was gone. I felt like her protector. To put it in context, this was a tiny eight year old girl who was protecting her mom. I think even as a parent right now in the thick of it with two teenage girls and a four year old boy I don't realize how much these kids need our love, affection, support, and attention.

I went to see my dad in the summer and found out I was getting a little sister. I loved babies and I always knew I would be a mom. But all of a sudden my dad says, "I am flying you to stay with your grandma and grandpa for the summer." How this felt to a little girl who didn't feel safe at home, now she doesn't feel safe at her second home because Dad's new family is more important than my sister and me. So when they say you need to feel love as a child from your parents, they are 100% correct! At this point in my life I had a huge wound from my mother and a huge wound from my father so the next person in my life, God rest his soul, was my stepdad. He was one of the sweetest men I have known, until he got a beer in his hand. This was the real reason I was afraid to leave my mom. Now I can comprehend that these were all broken people who were just trying to make life work. They all had not so great childhoods, how sad that so many of us can say that. They did the best they could with the tools they learned from their parents and stepparents.

I don't remember a lot from my childhood, though I remember a recurring dream I had that my grandma's pool (which she didn't have) was filled with blood. I hated the color red until about two years ago. I didn't realize that I was so hurt by my dad leaving me and my sister to go to California and start a new family until about eight years ago when I set out on my personal development journey. I do feel like the strongest, bravest people I know (or would like to know) have had the most pain in their lives and they grew from it. Just like Tony Robbins says, sometimes our worst days can become our very best days. We have the ability to not suffer in difficult situations and are able to bring light and happiness to others by sharing how we got through our trauma.

And rewind one more time. I got married at 22. There was no question in my mind that I wanted to marry this man. We got married on a beautiful day in September outside in a beautiful park. Fast forward a year and baby number one is on her way. She was very colicky and stressed us both out to our max. She cried 20 hours a day. The only time she didn't cry was when she had worn herself out and would sleep for about 15 minutes or if she slept in the crook of my arm. One night she woke up and the covers were over her face and I thanked God dearly for my motherly instinct, or my husband snoring so loud he woke me up. Either way she grew out of it and onto baby number two and I had a miscarriage the very day we moved into our brand new house. That house was just bad luck. The previous owners didn't tell us there was a huge leak in the front of the house and water was running into the basement. About a month after moving in it rained a ton and we opened the wall to discover an amazing amount of black mold, the kind they use to make antibiotics. My husband decided to put a fan on it to dry it out. I told him I thought it was mold, and he was sure it was just rotted wood. I didn't argue with him, and let that fan blow black mold spores throughout our house. A year went by and baby number three came along and we all started getting sick. I began nearly blacking out on a regular basis and went to a neurologist only to find out I was getting lesions on my brain and I might be at risk for multiple sclerosis. We both ended up at the pulmonologist because we were having trouble breathing and my husband was feeling depressed. He went to the Home Depot and bought a mold kit. Mold started growing almost instantly in our Petri dish. We called in a specialist to do a real mold test and he told us we shouldn't be living there, it wasn't safe.

We packed up to go stay with my mom for a couple weeks while we got our house fixed. Thank goodness my ex husband and his entire family are amazing at remodeling houses, I don't know how we would have afforded what would have been $30,000 in repairs – a huge amount especially with a two year old and a two month old. Shortly after we arrived at my mom's, my step dad ended up needing a place to stay too. OH WOW, JUST LIKE OLD TIMES. I could hear the two of them fighting even though they'd been divorced 10 years. Despite the trauma and PTSD triggered, I am glad to say we left the next morning for my mother-in-law's house, where we stayed for a month. My second baby finally stopped crying all of the time. Probably because she wasn't breathing in horrible mold. My oldest daughter developed allergies, but those are gone now. Most people think that allergies are the worst thing that comes from mold exposure. Let me tell you, they are absolutely not. We went to so many doctors appointments that year with unexplainable symptoms. I was having black outs randomly which is extremely scary when you have a four month old baby. The black outs stopped as soon as we moved out of the house.

Fast forward a few years to a Chiefs game day and the day my husband and I decided to tell the girls we were getting divorced. The worst day for the three of them and a very freeing day for me. When I type this or say this out loud it sounds terrible. We were all sobbing our eyes out and it was seriously the hardest thing I have ever, ever done. I'd felt stuck for a while, like I didn't even know who I was anymore. Now I know that the real reason is because I had no clue what love was supposed to look like. Let me tell you a little about how I learned this. It was a long journey, nearly 10 years in the making.

It all started when I was on my lunch break at work and I had driven over to a store nearby. I had called a life coach and she was returning my call. I told her about my story and what I was looking for and she blatantly said, "You need a therapist and some EMDR before you can ever work with a life coach." I thought, did this lady seriously just tell me that I am too screwed up to see a life coach?! Yep, pretty much that is exactly what she said and I am so thankful for her honesty. She gave me the name of a therapist named Jennifer. Oh man did I like her. We did EMDR together and our last session she looked at me and said, "Tricia you seem to be doing great. I don't think you need to come see me anymore." I was proud of my progress, and impressed that she didn't even want my money! I was on cloud nine, ready to find my person, because I was all healed. I had told her about this guy I was talking to and he seemed so perfect. We had been on the most amazing first date in history and didn't leave each other's side for like three days. We walked down to the neighborhood pool, hopped the fence because it was closed, dipped our feet in and had the most romantic night ever. This went on for about a week and then he disappeared. Not completely, just when it was convenient for him. So I checked out a little. This is my coping mechanism, if you haven't noticed yet. When things don't work for me I check out and move on. We kept seeing each other for a little while and I let him meet my girls. In hindsight I know it was way too soon and I take full responsibility for this decision. But at that moment, I was trying to make it work.

A couple of months went by and I saw on his Facebook page a woman comment, "well you didn't have a girlfriend two weeks ago." Astonished, having just learned I was pregnant, I realized my baby daddy was cheating on me with a girl who didn't even live in the same state. My partner and I decided to work things out; we probably should have just stopped the relationship there, but we didn't. He asked me to marry him soon after. I said yes and we got married.

We had our son Jackson and he has been the sweetest little boy ever. He is a true blessing, so I don't regret the situation at all. His dad and I were married for two years and there were a couple of things that happened that pushed me to finally realize he was not worthy of a relationship with me. He wasn't going to change anytime soon. The lies were not slowing down and the fighting wasn't getting any better. We separated in October. I much much too soon met another man and dove head first into a relationship. For all of my fellow single people out there, I know everyone says this, but you need at least a year of singleness with some intense counseling before you step in deep with a new person.

With this man it was so very different. He was exactly what I had been looking for. I thought, "wow I got so lucky I never have to date again." I was so in love with him. We found a wall decoration that said "my person" with a place to hang a picture (and I had the perfect one). My ex husband had started crap with the new boyfriend and I literally felt like I was living someone else's Lifetime movie nightmare.

I remember looking at my boyfriend at the ribbon cutting ceremony for my business and thinking, "mmmhhmm, that man's all mine and I am going to cherish him forever." Not too much time went by and despite many "I love you" texts, my person broke up with me. Have you ever thought your heart was going to stop beating because you were so heartbroken? I have never cried like that before. I remember driving home from work, but felt the urge to pass my house and just kept driving. My chest hurt so bad I thought my heart might stop. Not that I wanted it to, but I was crying so uncontrollably – something that had never happened to me before. My dream man told me I was his dream girl and showed me what it was like to be truly loved. The security that I felt with him was amazing. I had never in my life felt secure with another human before. In a blink of an eye that security and safety disappeared. He couldn't take the drama anymore and I wasn't doing anything about it, or so he thought. We were on again and off again for the next year.

Fast forward about six months and that amazing old boyfriend and I started chatting off and on. He Facetimed me on my way home from work one day. I saw his face pop up and thought, "oh here we go again. I am falling in love all over again." It is weird, but we fell in love over Facetime because I couldn't see him all that much in the beginning until he met my kids. The very first time we talked on the phone, I was sitting in bed with no makeup on and he Facetimed me. He had the most amazing voice and was just so handsome. I always told him, "you just look like home." To some people, home is a safe place. My home growing up was the complete opposite, so it can be a good thing or a bad thing. He replied, "come see me." He had moved to Arizona about six months prior. I knew it was over when he moved 1,200 miles away, yet in that moment, being the free spirit I am, I booked a free flight on Southwest Airlines departing the next morning. When I saw him the feelings rushed back, just like every time I heard his voice. I had seriously never felt a love this deep ever before. We had a great time on Friday and Saturday and then Sunday rolled around and he asked me about my ex husband. I thought oh shit I have to tell him that we gave it another shot. He blew up, though not as intensely as before. I told him just to take me to the airport because he said he never wanted to talk to me again. Talk about one of the loneliest points in my life; sitting at the airport four hours early waiting for a flight after losing the love of my life, yet again. I got home and he texted me to make sure I was ok, because he loved me just as hard as I loved him. We both knew it still wasn't over.

Fast forward a few months and I got a text message from him telling me he had moved home and was in Texas with all of his stuff, on the road to Kansas City. I literally dropped my phone and started crying. The message came as I was sitting with dear friends who immediately asked me what was wrong and I told them what was happening. I waited a few hours and then texted back asking what it meant for me/us? He said he didn't know. We talked later that night. I was sitting in my aunt's basement. It was so very nice of her to let me and my three kids live with her for a month while our brand new house was being built. I wanted to see him so badly so I made plans to go see him at his brother's house the next night when my kiddos were with their dads. I went and it was really awkward. What were we doing here again? I asked myself. Nothing had changed.

Another couple months went by and he called me again; he came over and we would rekindle our love for two days. Then, he started stepping back again and not trusting me. I told him it was time we just be done and call it what it is. Insanity is thinking that doing the same thing over and over and over again is going to produce different results. I haven't spoken to him since that time. I finally managed to not respond to his texts.

As I am writing this chapter, I just ended my relationship with my ex husband (again). He has changed, and for the better, but he's just not right for me. I feel fortunate that my current mantra is: May he be happy, may he be blessed, may he be loved. I truly do wish for him to be happy. Ultimately I know what is best for me and my kids and being with him just wasn't it.

As Christmas approaches and I am reminded that I am alone for yet another holiday, I am perfectly fine with this! Want to know why? Because I know that my person is just around the corner, waiting for me, helping me let go of the past and move on to the future. The next man I am with is going to be the ONE. I just know it from the bottom of my heart. My reason for telling my story is for HOPE. I want you to know there is always hope, and I wish all of you healing.

My story is not over. I want to tell you what's been going on behind the scenes over the last two years in my life. The main thing to emphasize is that I continued to repeat certain defeating behaviors over and over, which attracted men who were traumatized at some points in their lives. I knew there was something I hadn't healed from yet. I started going to counseling. One particular therapist was a true Godsend to people trying to heal their inner child. My inner child was crying out in all of these situations. Once I get to a point with a counselor or a coach when I don't have much to say, I know that our time together is done. I do think that people are put in your life for specific reasons and so I moved on. My takeaways from my time together with this therapist were that I was finding people with whom I could basically recreate my childhood. What I learned as a child is that love hurts and if it doesn't hurt then it isn't love. I can tell you I am 100% done with relationships that incur hurt. Love doesn't hurt, it isn't fearful, it isn't worry, it isn't negative in any way. Are my person and I going to fight? Yes we are, but love can be obtained in everyone's story. Though one important key to this puzzle is loving yourself and being in charge of self care.

I started working with an amazing Self Love Coach. She was learning Emotion Code and I let her train on me a little. We discovered some pretty cool things, which helped me let unnecessary emotions go. She introduced me to a program called UHPW (Unleash Her Power Within – a Tony Robbins immersion program) and I decided to book a ticket to UPW with Tony Robbins. I had heard of him before and after some video research, I was amazed by him and booked a ticket to do his first virtual UPW ever. I was living in my aunt's basement while we were waiting for our house to be built. I decided I was going to Cancun to do the virtual retreat, soaking up some sun at the same time. Despite the difficulty of getting to Cancun, Mexico, during COVID, I felt it very empowering to go to Cancun by myself, not to mention to have such a transformational experience. I had been reading, listening, and watching every personal growth message and book for the last eight years and this was a life changing experience. I then got a Tony Robbins personal coach who helped me work through some challenges for about six months; Carla has been a truly amazing inspiration. Shortly after I finished my work with Carla, I connected with a client Rachel, and we bartered services. I helped her on her website and she helped me with getting into alignment. One of her last pieces of advice was that I take a bath. We laughed at this; she wanted to clarify that she didn't mean I was dirty and needed to take a bath. Having been practicing self care now for some time, it was so eye opening. Another thing that happened during the time of our sessions is founding the Soul Setters' Collective. This is a way to bring together my web business and entrepreneurial spirit with personal growth and development. I absolutely know that I am now on the path God paved for me, and that I am serving my purpose at this point in my life. Rachel also said in our last session that I will feel so mad at myself for not taking care of myself sooner. So, I sit here typing at my desk and I can tell you what just happened was truly enlightening... After typing out my story, I sobbed. I now feel like this was the last piece of my healing puzzle and I am FREE to move along my path now. I am frustrated I didn't do this a long time ago, even if Rachel told me I would feel this way. The one thing her warning did is make me have grace for myself, that I didn't just know this was the missing piece.

I put my whole self on the line for you, so you can see the good, the bad, and the ugly - and hopefully relate to all parts. Another point I want to make is don't be afraid to ask for help. I would still be trying to work it out with one of my exes if I wouldn't have asked for help. I discovered that I was attracting people that were showing me I still had some healing to do. Let me ask you what do you need to heal?

"Thoughts produce an electrical charge and feelings produce a magnetic charge. Emotion is a record of past experiences."

~ Dr. Joe Dispenza

One thing I am so very proud of is teaching my kids all of the self development tools that I have learned. Here is a list that my daughter made in 2021.

Maci ~ things ive learned in 2021

1. You can't base your emotions all on one person. They can't be the reason you ruin your day or the reason you can't have fun when you're out with friends. Live your own life, feel your own feelings and find someone who actually makes you feel good.
2. Always trust your gut feelings. Always.
3. Make every single day different. Even the littlest step can add millions to your day. It'll help you not live on repeat.
4. Write.
5. Share your feelings. If you feel like they are too much for someone, you're not sharing with the right person.
6. Love yourself before someone else.
7. When you are hungry, find something to eat, even if your house has "nothing".
8. Don't listen to the bad things people have to say about you. It comes from a place of insecurity inside of them, it has nothing to do with you.
9. YOLO.
10. When you're with someone you shouldn't be jealous of who they talk to.
11. Not everyone or everything is permanent.
12. Counseling is good for you. Whether you think you need it or not.
13. Pray.
14. Always do what you feel is best for you, even if you lose some people.
15. If it makes you happy, who cares.
16. Talking about it is important.
17. Become the best version of yourself. No matter how long it takes, no matter the effort, find time to become the fullest version of yourself.
18. Give it time.
19. If someone leaves, don't chase. If they can't stay, it's not even worth

the thought.

20. If they did it once, they'll do it again.
21. Love, real love, takes sacrifice. If they can't sacrifice anything for you, they're not your love. Love never fails.
22. Don't fear the judgment of others when you do the things you want. Embrace it, do what makes you smile.
23. Wear that outfit you laid out to wear but are too tired to put on, it'll make you feel good.
24. Remember that waking up everyday is the biggest blessing. It shows that God isn't done with you quite yet, keep living each day to the fullest.
25. Consistency is key.
26. Happiness within yourself is more important than happiness from other people.
27. Laughing is the best medicine.
28. Set a routine.

"I am a business owner that is bringing together personal growth and business development. My vision is to celebrate fellow business owners on their journey. I am a constant work in progress. My focus is on being the best version of myself in my personal life and in business every single day."

≈ Tricia Keightley

CPSIA information can be obtained
at www.ICGtesting.com
Printed in the USA
LVHW081815040322
712652LV00003B/65

9 780578 353661